IDEAS and DISCLOSURES

notionpress.com

BOOK ONE OF IDEAS TRILOGY

IDEAS and DISCLOSURES

THIRUMAN ARCHUNAN

notionpress.com

Notion Press

Old No. 38, New No. 6

McNichols Road, Chetpet

Chennai - 600 031

First Published by Notion Press 2015

ISBN: 978-93-52061-97-6

Dedicated to

Love the daughter of nature,

Justice the son of reason and

God an intention of the mind.

Preface

This book is an attempt to express some of my thoughts on certain intimate, vital and eternal issues like *God, reason, intuition, love, the mind, nature, faith and religion* on which I am convinced. The title of book is ***Ideas and Disclosures***. The book as a whole is the result of my routine thinking that occurred during the course of work as well as outside of it. I would especially collect my thoughts during the lazy Sundays at home and also during my travels, which make mind lighter and less diverse. As I will articulate further on in the introduction, the *Ideas* are simple statements that have been created out of deliberate attempts to find an answer to my cerebral quest while the *Disclosures comprise of* different, new and revealing information on several issues. The *Ideas* obviously necessitated repeated thinking and hence more investment of time than the *Disclosures*. By *Disclosures* I intend to represent the practical facts and truths and the sudden revelation of arcane messages which did not call for much interpretation. I also feel the distinction I made between the *Ideas* and *Disclosures* is approximate and superficial; relevant only for this book title. As such I have not actually divided the book into two separate sections, one for *Ideas* and the other for *Disclosures*. Broadly, I can say that *the Ideas are mental conceptions and Disclosures are observed and heartfelt messages.* I would also leave it to the readers whether a particular thought is an Idea or a Disclosure!

While completing the book with my numerous and often contradictory thoughts, it turned out that the *reason*, *mind* and *God* have become the dominate themes. I personally have a very strong inclination towards these three and find them as inseparable elements of a conscious human mind. They are *ageless* themes warrant adequate *patience* to appreciate its relevance and worth.

It is expected that a particular thought, either the *Idea* or *Disclosure*, may be true and acceptable for someone or partly correct for others or fully wrong for yet another group of people. The human mind often rests firmly on subjective views and hence opinions are expected to differ. If an *Idea* pertaining to a particular issue is not acceptable it would only mean that it at least has one more opinion or interpretation.

I strongly believe today that in practical world the *reason* and *faith* have equal significance in individual preference and practice though as a young man I thought that *reason* was the only authentic way of interpreting this world. Hence many *Ideas* revolve around the reason and science on one side and faith and religion on the other.

There are few empirical *Disclosures* that originated due to the direct observations of real world incidents.

The book is definitely not intended for any particular target audience. It is essentially my thinking and beliefs that convinced me and I can only hope that it would also be acceptable to those who read it, at least to a reasonable extent.

The language of the book is simple so that it would make the *Ideas* easily understandable to a wider section of people.

Thiruman Archunan

July 2015

INTRODUCTION

This book deals with intimate, ageless and fundamental subjects like *God, reason, intuition, time, nature, design, love, accident, faith, fate.* It also deals with numerous day to day issues such as *good, bad, man, woman, lies, power, democracy etc*. In general the word *Idea* is a conception or conclusion that happens in the mind, as the result of one's thought process. I retain the same meaning here and hence each of the ***Ideas*** in this book is brought out after a deliberate attempt to define and understand a particular issue. As such the Ideas represent the mental conceptions with an investment of time, however short or prolonged it may be. However, certain knowledge happens in a flashing moment or as inner revelation without much mental processing. It simply happens and there is no intentional or deliberate attempt here except for some careful observations or remembrance. The ***Disclosures*** come under this category.

If I say '*a business is for survival and more business is for exploitation*' creation of this statement definitely involves some kind of mental activity correlating the very necessity for doing the business, the businessmen and the customer to exist, for exploitation! But if I think about *love my heart vibes the feeling first and the brain only captures it later without much interpretation*. The former is an *Idea* and latter is a *Disclosure*!

Except for the above mentioned broad and superficial distinctions meant for the title of this book title, the very content of the book is not organized separately as Ideas and Disclosures. The numerous *Ideas* and *Disclosures* are presented only in a random manner, thereby expecting the very randomness would create interest. Again, each *idea* can be read and understood as stand alone. A particular theme may get repeated because the same *idea* have been created to represent differing real world situations and perspectives; for instance the *reason* or *God* have been interpreted in numerous ways to capture and validate the various practical circumstances that any human mind itself would experience.

This book, conceived as the ***book one*** of the ***IDEAS*** *trilogy* only outlines the basic frame work of my thinking in the form of ideas and disclosures. As such the each thought is presented in simple and straight forward statements with brief explanations. In many cases strong and fundamental themes are deliberately presented in a *sharp* and *abstract* way considering that the brevity would maintain the beauty of the subject in question. However, the last few pages of the book conclude with elaboration of few thoughts of practical importance.

In this ***book one*** I have introduced an idea of two Gods. In one of the *ideas* I say: a man actually has *two Gods: the one that created him and the other he created*. I mentioned only some brief features of these two Gods. The enormous nature of the subject involving God obviously compels for an elaborate treatment necessitating another *two books*.

Therefore the next book, the ***book two,*** predominantly deals with the *second God* born out of the human mind; along with the 'second god' some ideas involving larger and substantial subjects like *accident and design, nature of this world, religion and science* have been dealt with.

Since the second God of the human mind occupies a considerable space of the ***book two*** along with other heavier issues like the nature of the world, reason and mind and numerous other day to day issues, I decided to go for the ***book three*** dedicated to the *first God* alone.

The *first God* is an authentic and undisputed entity and I conceived it more as a scientific theory than the man-made second God and hence anticipate an enormous labour, time and details. It would definitely involve considerable investment of time to bring out the first God in any convincing way. As such the ***book three*** is reserved only for *the first God that exists between man and nature.*

1. The world is *continuously discontinuous*. It is continuous for *intuition* and thinking; discontinuous for *reason* and observation. The human *senses* break it down but the unconvinced *mind* unites it.

2. Over the years, the *stories* that men created became more important and influential than the men themselves. Hence born are the *religions* and many others.

3. Man is not the owner of the *mind* but only a user. It is *nature* that owns mind; man hires only a small portion of it that too for a brief period!

4. Without *imagination*, humanity would have perished long back.

5. *Marriage* is the best compromise between *nature* and *culture*; it is a process where the reason and consciousness is on one side and instinct and intention on the other side. All of this ultimately concedes to the might of underlying desire.

6. Truth exists*: whatever a man and a woman are not able to tell is actually a truth!*

7. The *conscience* is a right mix of instinct, reason and culture. The conscience itself is not a truth but it has an ability to access the *truth*. Again conscience is assembled only by the *reason*, one of the constituents of the conscience.

8. *Human reason* is like a lighting *lamp* in a tower that glows at an elevation and hence has a better perspective to look at the things around. Yet the lamp sitting on the tip of the tall tower only knows the things that get illuminated

due to the falling of that very lamplight; the lamp cannot see the powering wire and towering mast because only the shadow falls on them. Hence the lamp forgets the existence of the wire that powers it and the tower that supports it. Similarly human reason is actually sitting on the tip of the mind; reason thinks as if it does everything as per its own choice and instruction by forgetting the supporting tower, the mind and powering wire which are the connections of the mind. The lamp and its glow would collapse with the tower the same way reason also will collapse when the human mind itself collapses. Therefore reason is never an independent authority but it only 'seems' to be independent in the back drop of day to day activities.

9. *Fear* of nature led to the creation of society. *Hatred* among men led to culture. *Envy* among women led to virtue!

10. *Accident* is nature's way of starting a *design*; design is man's way of looking at the accidents.

11. *Good* and *bad* are not of different kinds but only varying in degree; both vary in quantity not quality. There is nothing called quality but for a variation in quantity; a quality is an effect or result of certain proportions of various quantities. *Quality can never be an independent property. Quantity is primary and fundamental and quality is only secondary and derived.*

12. *Good and bad and society*: it is a known fact that both ***good*** and ***bad*** are not absolute but relative since they vary from society to society. But, the very *quantitative* nature of good and bad make it interesting: *if one does 'a good thing' repeatedly it will become a bad thing; again if he does 'a bad thing' repeatedly it will become bad thing*

only! This is because a *good* thing becomes bad at a limiting point that is known to us; but a *bad* thing has already become bad at a certain limit that is not known to us! But for the quantitative element, there is nothing inherently distinct in the good or bad classification by human beings. This compels us to come to an important conclusion: for any given society *firstly,* there should a border between the good and bad. *Secondly*, the border is such that if one looks from the side of good, there is a maximum quantity beyond which good always becomes bad. Similarly from the side of bad, there a minimum quantity equal to or below which bad is always not bad. The minimum may be zero also! *As such the good* and *bad* cannot be two fundamentally different or distinct things yet they seem to be distinct either for an individual perspective or for a group's social settings. This distinction matters for a large group of people to make their social interactions or very life itself meaningful. Again behind the *superficial distinction* of good and bad there exists always a connection that makes both as one and the same!

13. *Nature* takes the decision first, *man* only agrees, reconciles, modifies, refutes, contradicts etc., the decision subsequently. It means the application of *reason*, the discretionary power of man, only happens afterwards!

14. By *god* a man is afraid more of himself than anything else; every day he is struggling to construct a god first to suit himself and only then to others.

15. The usefulness of *wealth*, *status* and *power* either to possessor or otherwise depends only on a single factor: the nature and strength of the individual's *reason*.

16. If a man is ruined by a woman another woman would definitely save him; strangely the cycle never repeats and hence it is a one way process, another woman cannot ruin the same man!

17. *Nature* hides man many things; but *man* hides the nature itself. Nature decides when to show a man what; man decides what to the society how!

18. A man actually has *two Gods*. The one, *created him and* the other, *he created*. Nature is not the *first* God but the first God exists in and as a part of the nature; a man creates a God with the assistance of whatever *reason* he has against the forces of nature that are perceived to be as threat, hence the second God. The second God is the *property* of an individual mind that created it. I am quite clear about the *existence* of the first God and *implications* of the second God.

    All of us are witness to the facts that: one man butchers and sacrifices animals for the sake of God, whilst another one relishes the human corpse and yet another advocates not to turn towards even garlic. Then there are those who promote celibacy often *unsuccessfully* and so on; all these are the characteristic features of the second God created out of human fear, ignorance, innocence, cunningness, ambition and numerous other human emotions that arise in both physical and social settings; therefore the more authentic first God is nowhere in these scenes and settings created by the human mind in its everyday existence. Above all, there is a lot more confusion and misunderstanding between scientific minded people on one side and followers of all kinds of religions on the other. For instance, *the rationalist and atheists frequently get anger and annoyed because they keep scientific nature the first God in their mental background and apply their reasoning power to interpret the strange, ignorant, abnormal human behaviour of the common masses associated with the second God.*

A child has the first God but it has not developed enough reason to know its own God. Again the *fear* is not yet felt by the child hence its mind does not begin to create the second God! In case of a fully grown and mentally mature man *the first God is felt and known due to the fear ingrained in the instinct and the second God is the surrender and prayer brought out by the reason!* The ingrained fear dominates and confused human reason has no other alternative except to surrender. The creation of the second God is such a *tactful* way of surrender by a human mind.

In the world of humans a *conscious* mind often seeks God either tacitly or explicitly to protect from its fearful, incomplete and unguarded existence. If this plain fact is admitted as being true, there arises the following question: ***if God has to protect a man, then who and what threatens him and is yet capable of existing independent of the God?*** This question deserves an answer.

Throughout the human history there have been attempts to answer this question. This has resulted in confusion, contradictions, turmoil and beyond doubt fear. In fact, fear and its innumerable descendents ultimately lead to untold blind faith, manifold rituals in religion. To me answering this question directly results in the necessity to deal with the two Gods. I firmly believe that with combined support from *reason* and the *experiences of the human mind* this question can be answered in a convincing way.

As stated in the introduction, the second God will be further elaborated about in the *book two* of this series. The first God is subtle, scientific and natural but yet this has to be explored with substantial labour, hence will be dealt in book three. *The God mentioned at other places in this book only means the second God as perceived and created by humans in their minds and by society at large.*

19. *God* is as real as the human mind and his mind is as real as nature; which subsequently can be understood to be his own nature!

20. *A man's ego is valid only today; ego that existed yesterday and the ego that exists tomorrow do not count.* As a thought experiment, I assume that a *man as a continuous* entity and also the world always has kings and beggars. The king of today desires to trace his genealogy backwards and in the process he would be tending towards a beggar; similarly if a beggar of today does the same he would only end up as king! In their journeys the paths of both the curves have to meet and at that meeting point both the king and beggar would have the same status. They will meet the same fate if their curves of genealogy are traced into the future. *Ego makes a man to forget the time!*

21. *Life* is a mind's attempt to win over other minds, so along as it thinks the other minds are different from it.

22. Everything is as *real* as nothing, whatever the way 'nothing' itself is defined.

23. If an educated man fears, he is yet to be educated; it may be the case of either the man is naturally inadequate or *education* itself is insufficient, or sometimes even both!

24. Human *life* is a series of mistakes justified by *reason;* there is no escape from it since the reason is the first mistake born out of a process subsequently understood as the very life by the very reason!

25. *Spiritualism* exits only for individuals. *Reason* is born when two men decided to work together; the addition of more and more member necessitates the spreading of reason and this culminates in *culture*. Hence a culture is as dynamic as reason. The nature of the reason is the nature of the *spirit* within them for some men or nature of the *instinct* for some others.

26. Wherever and whenever a *woman* is harassed, abused and exploited, there exists either a religion or some kind of *irrational belief* and *suppression of reason* among the minds of men and women who are responsible for the exploitation.

27. When today's stupidity joins yesterday's stupidity it becomes a *myth*; by myth stupidity glorifies itself without leaving any chance to human reason!

28. The strength and weakness of *reason* is that it imposes a uniform way of thinking and understanding. Hence its usefulness is immediate to society but not to same extent and not to all of the individuals in the same society. The very fact that evolution happened at different geographical isolations made individuals with different levels of mental capacity; the *uniform force* of reason of society threatens individuals' minds that are not fully evolved to grasp the

reason. Such minds are weak and have only attained a capacity to create questions but are not able generate answers. Having created the questions they are ready to receive any answers instead of understanding the reason. The reason, for them, is a day to day struggle while religion is available as readymade stuff. Hence at the level of society, reason wins but at the individual level of practice reason often fails and that makes religion win.

29. *Love* is a discovery, *God* is an invention! The former is a manifestation and the latter is a creation.

30. *Nature* never allows *man* to understand it, however intelligent he thinks he may be. It tempts him by offering reason an initial success only to seduce and pull him on its side once for all. Finally man is left to sing the irrational songs of nature! The initial success is nothing but the overture of reason itself by nature. But even for a few men of wisdom, it takes years to conceive that the reason as part of nature while the majority continue to think that reason is independent of nature.

31. The greatest intellectual achievement of men should be not only in understanding the importance of *reason*, but to consciously and boldly overthrow it as and when the welfare of others' warrants it. Why should anybody think about others? This is because reason's practical worth is only with respect to others. *Instinct* is often enough to take care of an individual, but *reason* is necessary to meet the societal requirements and also to derive benefits from it.

32. Originally, *god was to save the individual mind from despair if not disaster, love was an attempt by one mind to possess another mind* and *justice was one mind's concern*

for all other minds. In case of first, the mind is too weak to understand itself. In the second, the human mind is not allowed to understand itself! In the third situation, the mind is on its own and does what is possible and what may be construed as the best with respect to the other minds.

33. Men are forced to think rationally and live irrationally because the poor *mind* is constantly torn between *reason* and *instinct*.

34. There is no *dharma* greater than a word uttered by a man of conscience; there is no *ḳarma* greater than a man listening to himself! Since an *intention* precedes action, it should be the reference point for action. The dharma and karma have to be interpreted and understood with the aid of the intention, word and action, and also in that order. The *intention* happens first and therefore it has been influenced least by human reason. The *words* carry a lot of intention and yet may be tainted by the cunningness of reason that is known to his conscience. The actions are under the influence of reason to a large extent; thus the actions are inferior to both intentions and words. Therefore karma precedes dharma and is more original than dharma! Karma is subtle, closer to nature and its infinite networks. But dharma is very much accessible and understandable to *reason* and therefore to his conscience.

35. The mighty *reason* renders only little help in understanding a *woman*!

36. *Mathematics* is the only beauty that has got independence from the human *senses*. Each science starts with a framework that is furnished by the human senses.

However, in case of mathematics *alone* some of the pure mathematicians' claim it as purely *abstract* and *mental* and hence free from the senses-based empirical world. Among other things, the familiar and simple examples they cite for this kind of reasoning are the *triangle* or *circle*. They say with a strong conviction that a mind can perceive a triangle independent of this physical world and that the sum of three angles of the triangle is always 180 degrees; similarly they have the same fixed belief that a circle can exist in the mind independent of this phenomenal world. Unfortunately both the arguments are not correct and not in accordance with what happens in the real world: without the aid of senses nobody can perceive measurement of angles *the way* it is now done and hence this kind of triangle is not a possibility; again for any measurement there should be a *reference* and a blind man cannot create a reference. Even if the blind man makes any such reference he cannot make it understandable to others, either blind or otherwise. In case of a circle also same situation persists: the ratio of circumference to diameter involves measurements. What really happens in the case of mathematics is that the *mind*, with a little familiarization of the sense-based objects and understanding, quickly idealizes and makes mathematics independent of human senses; that quick detachment of human mind from 'sense' dependence makes mathematics free from real world prejudices and that imparts beauty to mathematical objects.

37. Human *reason* has an ability to create mentally good things yet also paradoxically it is incapable of owning them and strategically it does not intend to own! Hence all such good things, including god, get independence as

soon as they are created. *The doomed yet tricky reason is left longing alone only to own its own creations!*

38. A Man has to necessarily create a *God*, as long as he does not know who created him.

39. A man's courage originates in his *conscience*; all other sources only produce cowards.

40. An *average human* mind is often torn between all kinds of extremes created by society. This makes life itself as eccentric, unbalanced and more often a vulnerable one for them. The propositions of *science* and *religion* are such that men made extreme theories and rules troubling the mind of the common man; such minds fail to understand the fact that a more satisfactory life lies somewhere in between *science* and *religion*. An optimal mix and better usage of both for an individual and for a society is very much a possibility, if one understands science and its inherent *limitations* and religion and its unwanted *excesses*.

41. Originally the *rituals*, particularly in the sphere of religion, were human reactions to the unknown aspects of nature to ward off fear. However, subsequent developments have transformed its nature and usage. One can always find in the evolution of human civilization, among other things, a stage in which religious *rituals* are used by men to subjugate women. Men and women are differently endowed by nature; men are rough, forceful and physical at least when young but in general women are practical, sensible and natural all through their lives. These, naturally useful and functional endowments of women seem to be a mismatch for some men whose reason was *cunning*; the reason first germinated among men and

its interpretation of human relations was to satisfy their cunningness. *Reason in its initial stage is always cunning only in later stages it performs social service.* I strongly feel rituals that are, originally created in religion started being misused by those men to manage the said perceived mismatch. Since women are more mental than physical it became necessary for men to create an imaginary and yet convincing but never to be proved ideas and stories so that women do not acquire any *reason*. *A man wanted, even now wants a woman to be as natural as possible. A woman with reason is a threat to most men.* He needed some neutral tools to achieve his purpose. Rituals correctly fit the bill. Rituals have been designed accordingly to connect human beings and God. By rituals men were able to control women by easily shifting the responsibility to God. Again when a woman acquires *reason*, a man becomes no match for her; knowing this a *man tries to keep the reason with him and hand over the rituals to women!*

42. *Nature* actually enlightens man on one side and fools him on the other side; it does so simultaneously; but fortunately a man feels as if it happens at two different times, and unfortunately even if he is aware, he cannot do anything to set it right; being a part of nature, it handles him the way he cannot understand it.

43. A man in his relationship with *nature* whatever makes him happy is declared as *design* and unhappy as an *accident*!

44. *Reason* is like fire and its usage depends on the user. Unless tamed and directed regularly, the reason would behave like wild beast. As such even tamed reason,

despite being a friend, can occasionally threaten the possessor.

45. A *man* is still ninety-nine percent animalistic and one percent cultural. Again, he will not hesitate to disown the one percent if it is a hindrance to his own desire and happiness. A man is an animal except during the brief periods of justifications he does for his own actions and that too differently at different times!

46. C*ulture* is often the thick coat a man wears for others, but for him it remains only as a dangling thin veil constantly swinging to the force of wind called passion.

47. In the court of *reason* man is always a claimant and *god* is always the respondent. The original intention for creation of God is to make him a respondent as and when the need arises. Hence when a man is in trouble his reason tries to save him by acting as an arbitrator; the reason sitting as sole judge asks the man for his claims and makes god to respond.

48. Religion, science, philosophy are basically *different ways* a man can look at himself.

49. To be *sacred* one has to hide a thousand facts; for some men, for the reason only known to god, it becomes a full-time job during the course of their lives!

50. Culture is largely man-made behaviour to protect and guarantee at least minimum satisfaction of the *basic instincts* of human beings while *ethics* involves the use of reason.

51. We know *ethics* as expected behaviour from members of any society. But somehow due to innumerable reasons,

both social and biological, a man for all practical purposes treat the ethics as an expected behaviour for all others except from himself. If the men of society are divided into '*poor*' and '*rich*' then they can be further grouped into either '*stupid*' or '*intelligent*'. Thus these divisions eventually make four different categories of men. One, the 'poor-stupid' second the 'poor-intelligent' third the 'rich-stupid' and the fourth ''rich-intelligent'. Here is how these categories view and follow *ethics* the most expected behaviour from any one. If a 'poor' man is 'stupid' he cannot make up any ethics either for himself or for others, after all he is poor and also stupid. The only choice for him is to follow the ethics created by others groups; he selects the rich and stupid and copies the behaviour of 'rich-stupid'. It suits him better because being poor he often aims to become rich than intelligent. One can witness in real life that 'rich stupid' men are always surrounded by predominantly by 'poor stupid'.

52. If a '*poor*' man becomes '*intelligent*', the most unfortunate yet not uncommon, he has to consciously follow some *ethics* for the sake of others while his intention is actually not to follow. He has to follow because he is poor, but he has no intention to do so because he is intelligent. His behaviour is more due to a social compulsion than voluntary choice; for him none of the groups are worth emulating; because the 'poor stupid' have nothing to offer him, the 'rich stupid' do not impress him because they are stupid, and he does not also like the 'rich intelligent' because of the 'rich' attached with that group!

53. If a '*rich man is stupid*', which is the most likely situation in any civilized society, he creates ethics only for others,

mostly to his supposed followers and the lower counterpart the '*poor-stupid*' as mentioned earlier. He does not indent to follow the ethics created by him, after all he is rich and also stupid; again the 'poor-intelligent' do not heed to him because the former is intelligent enough to know the tricks of latter. Hence the 'rich stupid' has to necessarily create ethics for the consumption of the 'poor-stupid' at least to ensure a working relation with them. It is these two categories that provide or create a huge possibility for a master and slave relations. But as minds evolve and progress, most of the social tensions crop up because of the relations between these two categories. We are still left with one more category the 'rich intelligent' the microscopic minority; this is because rich man can hardly ever become intelligent if he does not possess this quality, intelligence, in the first place! But an intelligent man can become rich only if he desires so! Hence this group is obviously a minority. Again, if a man is 'rich and intelligent' he is not constrained by any body's expectations; he does what he wants and some of his attitudes automatically turn out to be the *ethics* for others in society.

54. The *difference* and also the *connection* between *religion* and *science* are like the one between the *living* and *non-living*. In both the cases the things are totally different at a macro level, but at a micro level both become inseparably the same. For instance, all living forms survive by feeding on non-living forms and that points to the fact that there is an organic relation between them. Thus the distinction between 'living' and 'non-living' is superficial.

55. The distinction between living and non living arises due to a large scale ignorance of the very working of nature.

The world is fundamentally *continuous* and hence to talk of a *living* thing as a different and independent entity from a *non-living* thing is an immature way of understanding the very nature of both entities.

56. *Reason* is the greatest *discretion* a man can have. It is like a fire, most often like a wild fire. If he learns to tame and domesticate it, it would serve him like an obedient servant. But taming reason is not an easy task since the very taming itself has to be done only with the help of reason. Reason controlling reason is a mystery within the reason; however reason can be overpowered. Often *Nature* does that job through man, example the 'love'!

57. *Senses* are the gate way to nature; they have more or less nothing to show the mind about nature. The mind always uses these gates first to enter, only dump them, the senses, subsequently in favour of its own better routes, in the form reason, faith, intuition etc..

58. More than anything else it is the inherited *habits* that fool men repeatedly.

59. *Scientific truths* are truths in isolation; they are truncated and partial.

60. *Nature* is misunderstood and *habits* are often misleading; but men create *hope* in between them and pass on the life process.

61. The *Vedas, the ancient Indian scriptures* are far ahead of rational science. What the science is going to do for many centuries down the line was revealed in the *Indian Scriptures* many centuries past. The *theory of nature* is already out; only experimental verification is pending for the science of future.

62. *Good* and *bad* work at least at three different levels: at the *individual*, *societal* and *temporal levels*. For an individual they are different at different times and also in relation with different people. Among societies they are different for different societies. When considering a time scale, the good and bad are always varied within a same society. No doubt the good and bad are useful, but they as local as in their usefulness.

63. The concept of *Infinity* and *Zero* is the most basic fabric of nature. Interestingly both are one and same and the only *reality*. They are natural and invisible to human senses, but are very much within the reach of human intuition; both infinity and zero seem to exist at extremes of a continuum only because of our everyday experience of discreet things and numbers. Something that vibrates infinitely is zero and vice-versa. A man cannot look at an object that vibrates with infinite frequency, because it looks transparent. Objects are turn out to be ultimately vibrations from the perspective of experiment and perception. Infinite vibrations make things invisible. Infinity is not something mysterious, but it exists in an invisible way. Hence *invisible seems to be void or nothing, but actually it is everything; it is a potential source of everything.*

64. For a man to understand his *Self*, he has to negate many things including *God.* If he still requires a 'God' then he is yet to understand himself. Anybody can have a doubt about the very existence of God, but once he becomes certain about it, then it cannot be something external to him.

65. Every day the women in this world do thousands of *sacrifices* and also an equal numbers of *sins*. But the cause of all these is due to the demands that arise from *average* nature of men. On *average*, compared to women, men are *average* by nature!

66. A man's world revolves around his *intention*. Who is the *cause* of that intention? If he is the cause; who is he? If *somebody* beyond him is the cause, again who is he? And in what way is he related to that somebody? Without answering these questions one's mind is incomplete; the incompleteness makes the mind jump from one stand to another endlessly.

67. *Understanding* is heaven; *misunderstanding* is hell. Unfortunately by understanding the misunderstanding a man is always in between the hell and heaven.

68. Whatever exists, exists only for *you*. The same is never exists for all others. Real is *subjective;* anything *objective* is a manmade illusion.

69. There is nothing called a *Nothing*. Any nothing is always something.

70. There is no *objectivity* of any kind in this world. Whatever is seen, perceived, learnt, and understood are all one's own creations, conditioned by one's own attributes and the inevitable interpretation that follows.

71. The world is as *secret* as a man. His own secret makes him rather fools him into believing that the world is secret; there exists no secret beyond man.

72. It is understandable that something is *visible* and some other things are *invisible*. But every time it is the invisible

things that make the visible things manifest and hence the reverse also has to be true. In other words what a man *perceived* and what he thinks he has not perceived are all actually perceived by him!

73. Barring some sages and soothsayers, women are by nature far more *intuitive* than men. A woman always stands closer to *nature* than a man and his distorted reason.

74. Broadly speaking the human *mind* develops in *three* stages: one, it learns from other men and materials. This is the initial stage. Second, it behaves for others' sake. It gives more importance to what others think than its own. These two stages are inferior to the third stage in that the mind looks at itself. Most do not reach or do not want to reach the third stage because the mind looking at itself will be confusing if not self-threatening. Though the third stage seems difficult, fearful and unpleasant initially, *real life* exists only in the third stage. Hence it is prudent for any man to reach the third stage early and spend most of his life span in it!

75. The *holiness* of human social life depends entirely on the *genuineness* of one man's relationship with another man; that genuineness cannot be found in temples, churches or in mosques but in one's inner nature i.e., by listening to his own mind, each man can have sufficient access to his *instinct* and subsequently accumulate enough *reason* to understand what is holy and hence virtue and happiness. The inner nature is a hard nut to crack but human reason with repeated attempts can temper it first and subsequently even change it irreversibly.

76. On the whole there is no loss and no profit; the local issues finally dissolve and vanish into the *whole* without any distinction.

77. Despite the negligible life span, man tries his level best to achieve what he *desires*. This is done mainly, more than anything else, by fighting against himself! This is a peculiar trait, which I doubt any other animal or creature anywhere in the universe has. The *desire* itself is natural since there are a lot of instinctive elements in it; but to make *it* as the major cause of life is the handiwork of human *reason*.

78. Today, the most difficult thing for a man to do is to behave *normally*. This is because all normal qualities have been distorted by *extreme materialism* and *pseudo* spiritualism.

79. Whether a man likes it or not, or is it possible for him or not a *normal behaviour* is god's most expected attitude from a man.

80. *Materialism* as frequently leads to *inhuman* attitudes as spiritualism leads to *exploitation*.

81. In *capitalism*, material is more important than man and the materials handle men more than men handle the materials; it makes a man slave of materials and the beauty of his own *mind* is permanently unavailable to him.

82. I have always wanted to find out the superiority between *love* and *justice* since my young age; after wasting many years, it was only recently that I found out that both are one and the same! It is one and the same thing that appears in the form of love sometimes and justice at other times.

83. *Love* is sponsored by nature, the same way *justice* is sponsored by reason and *god* by a human mind.

84. The seat of the *mind* cannot be the brain, both logically and also actually because the mind exists outside the brain. The brain and any other body part acts as receptors and transmitters of the mind, which exists everywhere.

85. *Beauty* takes a man to some limit. *Talent* takes him to another limit. *Intelligence* takes him to yet another limit. But controlling the *mind* only takes him to a location farther than all the other limits.

86. Reason is always the prime suspect as no one would have created a *culture* to ever fight with the *nature*.

87. The childhood can be defined from birth to his awareness of death. During this period children are unaware of *God*. These events, both the awareness of death and the mind's initial attempts towards the invention of God take place within a close interval of time. Slowly and steadily a man is led to a stage where he is condemned to invent God and to justify it. *Every man does it and hence god is man's cheapest invention.* He creates in such a way that it is always acceptable to him. Interestingly, as he grows up he makes additions and alterations to his own invention to suit his own way of existence. He never dislikes, but only modifies, as he always needs it.

88. *Men* are not just a mechanical collection of electrons, protons, quarks etc. There is *purpose* behind it, however small, local or imperfect it may be; if a man is not responsible for such a purposeful collection the *nature around him* should be responsible, however blind it may be!

89. A man always keeps *God* above him to avoid any other man to lay claim to the post!

90. Two intelligent men never like each other; the same is the case with two foolish men. All preach truth which is the same, yet one can never see two sages or priests together, if any exception is found it will be only for the limited purpose of exploitation! *The differences among men make them naturally compatible and socially attractive!*

91. *God* is mind's internal reaction to some *external circumstances*. Here the external circumstances are as important as, if not more important than, the God itself!

92. From the perspective of *nature* there exists no difference between living and non-living things. But from the perspective of human beings to say less is better; one man claims that with the help of his mental or yogic powers he can stop the motion of planets; another man claims that his life is being strictly ruled by the very same planets. Nature has no *reason* hence there is no body to correct and guide these funniest of creatures called human beings.

93. The *truth* is never within the bounds of reason; but definitely exists close yet just outside its boundaries! Therefore, without overcoming reason a truth cannot be authenticated.

94. *Woman* is the song of *nature* and *man* is the dance of *reason*.

95. Naturally one cannot separate *soul* and *body*. The Soul is a sum total of its surroundings that imparts shape, qualities and attributes to what we understand and perceive as a thing or object. They are always connected

organically or otherwise. Accordingly, when death happens one cannot observe the escape of the soul; the question of escaping does not arise. Again, after death the apparently decomposed and disintegrated body cannot go anywhere without being surrounded by the soul that as a sum total of everything exists everywhere. In this context also there is no basic difference between *living* and *non-living*.

96. Everybody knows some kind of *truth* and that truth exists only for his mind; the real issue is not the existence of truth and awareness but how best a man is able to cope with it; the truth is beautiful only within that mind but in the practical world it is a day to day struggle.

97. A man can exist without god but god cannot do so without a human mind!

98. Between *good* and intelligent, good and beauty, good and wealth, good and power one should always select good alone. But to find what is good one needs *knowledge*. The knowledge only enables one to distinguish good from bad. Hence knowledge itself has to be necessarily good; that way the only reliable good is the knowledge since all others are subject to the scrutiny of knowledge. Here the question of where to find knowledge should not lead to a vicious circle. Whatever *ends* in good is all knowledge but it always comes at the end of a lesson!

99. *Rituals* are stupid man's way of managing his life. The stupidity makes him fearful and *fear* makes him ritualistic. But the real issue is not stupidity, it is about life! The stupidity already has its own interpretation and hence it works. As such rituals make chemical changes among

unintelligent, force their minds in a particular direction and thus definitely yield results, but only to a limited extent!

100. The very ideas of *equality* amongst men and women originated predominately from local social compulsions and often go against the basic nature of human beings; *the idea of equality is essentially an impatient interpretation of reason. It kills the sublime nature of beauty and purposes 'seemingly' implanted by nature.* Hence equality is an idea as useful or as useless as any other time-bound ideas of the reason.

101. *Equality*, even a stupid man will not say so if no other special circumstances are forcing him; these men made circumstances stifle reason and the natural feelings to promote a false sense of human satisfaction. *The intention and purpose behind the very formation of society and its subsequent long term benefits should have been derived only by the existence and awareness of 'inequality'. Respecting inequality is often more prudent than fighting for equality. The notion of love, the most beautiful of all earthly events, arises and becomes sustainable only due to the automatic acceptance of the inherent inequality provided by nature.* There is no place for equality in love but natural compatibility. A sustained love shows perfect compatibility of both the mental and physical world of those involved. Men and women are different and also complementary to each other even in mental feelings and physical facts; they do not interpret physical events in a same way. As such in between men and women inequality is the rule. Blind nature expects men to respect this basic fact and forces him to form a society; hence the society has its origin in inequality. *Nature never*

creates any two things as equal. No two things can be identical and hence never equal. No doubt the men and women are not things, but from the perspective of nature there is no difference between living and non-living! The existence and sustenance of inequality is the *first law of creation* of this phenomenal world from the perspective of human beings. *Escaping from the bare facts of inequality is mischief created by human reason; the reason tries to approximate, average and make it 'even' the feelings of individuals for the purpose of sustaining an opportunistic arrangement called as society; but how far each individual varies from the 'average' is not accounted for by the same reason; many social ills breed from the indifference of reason to this fact.*

102. Between *power* and *money* or wealth, power is more natural and superior; accumulation of money is weak men's indirect way of acquiring the same power and hence inferior.

103. If everything is changing, there should be something unchanging or permanent. The good and bad, man and woman, white and black, tall and short, etc., one cannot exist, both logically and practically, without the other; the one is not conceivable without the other. The same yardstick should be applicable to something that undergoes *change* and a *permanent* one. *The change is inconceivable without a permanent entity.* It seems that change happens only in the physical world and the permanent entity is only a mental construct. If existence of the permanent entity cannot be proved, the idea of change also has to be buried! *Even if change is local in character, there should be something locally permanent!*

104. The underlying feature of *democracy* is not really the freedom of the individual as anybody would think first, but it is an intended and also a broad based mischief. *Democracy* is a playground of fools; deceit and exploitation are the only two rules of the game. Men are mischievous by nature and the same is due to biological and sociological reasons in their genes and courtesy of evolution. Democracy satisfies this nature of men by ensuring opportunities for everyone. This single important feature imparts the sustainability necessary for democracy.

105. The chief advantage of *democracy* is that, it ensures *power* to the stupid and *freedom* to the intelligent. The democracy is neither better nor the best yet it is a successful arrangement for the 'majority' while the 'minority' manage themselves.

106. The freedom in *democracy* is only to ask questions, not to get any answers; the *power* is never powerful enough to answer because it is closely associated with stupidity. The freedom in *autocracy* is only to receive answers, without any questions being asked. In *autocracy* one man spoils many and in *democracy* the same becomes individual responsibility!

107. *Freedom* kills more people than war; democracy is the proof.

108. A *wrong* route can never be a long route; but the lesson is learnt only at the end of the road!

109. *Imperialism* is exploitation from outside while *nationalism* is the same within; all are different faces of same human nature that never changes.

110. A man's *activity* represents one of the infinitely possible sample manifestations of the *nature* surrounding him.

111. *Women* are naturally social and *men* are social in nature.

112. A *perfect woman* exists; but she will get angry twenty five times in twenty four hours!

113. *Education* of women is the best means to understand them while subjugation only leads to serious misunderstanding. Education makes *women* manifest their true nature and thus makes men's' jobs less difficult!

114. Something is declared as *matter* only after a stamp of space and time imprinted on it by *senses*. If time is subjective and also space does not really exist then the nature of matter is just left to anybody's guess.

115. *Physics* first makes a cut in nature; again what it explains is only the cut not the nature itself.

116. The difference between *animal* and *man* is the latter wastes a lot of time to prove that he is not the former! Often unsuccessfully.

117. What a *man* does today was originally intended in some corner of his mind when he was younger than 18 years old, however faint it may be!

118. *Art* is a useless mind's useful creation.

119. A *stupid* person thinks that every following day will be happier compared to today; but still the *stupider* people think that every other day may be awful like today!

120. There is no knowledge without *patience*; real *destruction* starts when a man repeatedly fails to listen to his own mind.

121. *Ignorance* is the motive force of life; hence each man is ignorant in his own way!

122. *Philosophy* makes a lazy man active and an active one lazy.

123. Whatever a man doesn't know or cannot know or is not allowed to know but is just only aware of tends to have an *authority* on him!

124. *Nature* never gives *freedom* to a *man*; the so-called freedom is an intelligent man's way of being foolish!

125. Man creates *god* and often destroys it only to create again. It is an endless cycle produced by the peculiar combination of human *consciousness*, *reason* and *belief*. The consciousness always exists, the destruction and creation regularly takes place according to the strength and weakness, respectively of human *reason*. When the strength of reason is not sufficient then the man-made *belief systems* along with *natural passion* within him push aside 'the insufficient reason'; now the *belief* dictates the man as how to behave: it first asks him to create a *God* then tells him about the rest.

126. An individual's *life* and hence his *understanding of life* is a trial and error process; during the trial and error, one is bound to face many challenges, mismatches, discrepancies, gaps or incompleteness with respect to the concerned mind's expectations. Often the trial process becomes longer than a human life span. In such circumstances in order to complete the trial the concerned individual makes suitable assumptions. With the help of these assumptions the man set rights the discrepancies and gaps.

One man fills the gap with *god*, the other did not find any scope for god, third uses or dump the god according to the changing necessity of the trial itself, the fourth did not want to fill the gap but keep extending the trial till his death and so on. What is interesting for any individual is that not only the trial is inevitable but at the end the trial is always found out to be correct!

This is because, firstly, a man with a *mind* and consciousness has to *necessarily* undergo the trial process; there is no escape from it. In the trial process *the mind tries to know everything without knowing itself*; it is only at the final phase of trial the mind knows itself to some extent. Secondly, since all men conduct their *own* trial with their own mind, each trial is unique and becomes mind specific. No one cross checks with another's minds because it is not feasible for one mind to cross check another. Hence the very trial process happens in isolation but everyone only compares the outcome of the trial, the *result*. The result makes one as *theist*, another as *atheist* and yet another as a *sceptic*. Again every one justifies his trial because the very trial process had already provided the justification! That justification lends man a satisfaction. Hence *an individual's life is a trial, justification and satisfaction in that order!*

127. A man's troubles have their origin either in the *excess* influence of power, wealth etc or *deficiency* of the same. The troubled man starts to rely more on his *intuition* than *reason;* the trouble shows him that his own *reason* so far gave only a partial picture of the world outside while intuition renders a better picture of his individual human nature. Hence the man in trouble becomes more prudent

and musters enough courage to either manage or even forgo the attractive extra attachments like status, wealth etc. in favour of retaining and cultivating the intuition further.

128. The value of *intuition* as an asset often lies low due to the impact of capitalism. Intuition *is a subtle feeling, an instruction a calm mind receives; it is more natural than reason; also at individual level it is more useful than reason*. In the real world it is a fact that *women* manage adverse circumstances better than men; for the sake of mental peace, a woman would forgo the wealth etc. more *quickly* and *naturally* than a man can do; a man does slowly as he has to overcome the *reason*, the great justifier. In case of men, the frequent use of reason and their materialistic, scientific bent of mind coupled with adventurous attitudes veil the intuition that exists within them; women are already *mental* and hence have quick access to intuition. *Simply put, women are more intuitive than men; what a man searches and struggles for days at a time, a woman finds out in seconds.*

129. An average mind thinks all *problems* have their origin outside of it; even a matured mind shifts parts of the blame out of it to external sources. But the problems are the very *mind's* way of functioning; it cannot function without a problem. For instance - *If a man meets someone he may like or dislike that someone and if he does not meet any one he may like or dislike himself.* This is the way any normal human mind functions. Some kinds of problems are necessary for a mind to give a direction to itself and hence his life. Hence, problems give a man an ability take decisions and that decision shows the man

the way forward. *The directionless mind is boring and hence men work throughout their life only hoping to get the right direction at each instant!*

130. *The mind*: the working of the human mind is not fully known and whatever we know also seems to be strange! *The very working of mind is actually a series of changing mental states;* each man's changing mental states are understood as the working of his, completely unique and highly individualistic mind. The changing mental states happen either *naturally* or due to human *volition* or due to the both; but due to the very the existence of consciousness and reason the changing mental states are captured as a concerned man's decisions or judgments at each instant. However, the reason tries to own only those decisions that are useful to it including the ones that happened *naturally!*

131. *The problems and the solution:* if a human mind has a taken a decision it simply means it has solved a problem. Strangely *for the human mind a solution to a problem can also turned out to be a problem!* But it happens as time passes. Initially it seems true that a mind found a solution with respect to a particular problem; but as time progresses the mind is exposed to many other perspectives; now with respect to one or more of these new set of perspectives the solution again becomes a problem, even if the concerned the man is not aware of it immediately.

    Therefore in life *the mind actually goes from one problem to another while the concerned man thinks that he has solved the problems one by one!* Above all everything looks meaningless without defining what actually the ***problem is*** or what the ***solution*** really is. The very working of the mind shows him that it is not possible to have *separate* definitions, one for the problem and the other for the solution; this is because *a problem never remains a problem and the solution never remains a solution but for a brief period of illusion*. But there is an escape route: simply define the *mind itself as a problem and then the man will have a solution. The human mind is a problem in itself and hence the very existence and its functioning are understood only through such problematic existence. In the real world a man may panic without a problem/challenge and hence even if nobody creates a problem, his mind creates its own problems out of nothing and keeps with it!*

132. Even today a *man* retains 99 percent of animal qualities; the balance 1 percent consists of distorted reason in the name of *science* and *logic* and blind beliefs in the form of *religion*. Strangely, the minority one percent helps to manage the mighty mind and pass the time span called *life*!

133. A man's *desire* happens instantaneously, and reason understands it only later. The desires have a complex origin and the social, economical, rational, irrational and biological elements are all present in a man's desire; though the biological element is immediate and more understandable to him than the other elements. The rational and other components are gradually imbibed into the biology of men and act from the external settings where a man lives.

134. *Prostitution or promiscuousness* amongst women is largely due to instinct than poverty and any other external circumstances; citing the poverty etc., as causes are weak

justifications brought out subsequently. It is strange that in all societies predominate causes of social behaviour are often unexplained and kept at the background!

135. *Freedom* is a dangerous customer to handle by common men. A man of high practical prudence or a man who is able to balance *experience*, *reason* and *religion* only can handle it in any useful way for either to him or for the society in which he lives. If this is known to many, they would not question the existence of *religion* among the masses. Any religion tacitly intends only to clip a man's freedom; it is a *submission* of one's mind without resorting to reason every time. It is not that the religious masses do not have reason but they do not want reason; in other words they do not want *freedom*; the religions somehow make common men believe that their freedom leads their minds to unchartered territories where fear and uncertainty threaten their insufficient reason. When the reason is weak the concerned man feels himself to be unstable and insecure!

136. Human *life* is a continuous process of understanding his misunderstandings. Whatever a man now understands is actually a misunderstanding that would definitely become clear from the subsequent understanding of the same. The same way this latest understanding also turns out to be a misunderstanding next time in future! Then why at all he should venture into the futile territory of understanding? There is some worth at the end of the long process: ultimately a man's knowledge is nothing more than his understanding of all his earlier misunderstanding.

137. Understanding our own limitations, both physical and mental, is also a kind of *enlightenment*.

138. *Art* is a man's attempt to present a scene in between the *instincts* and *culture*. A man's imagination goes up as the culture progress, at the same time he puts a restriction on his instincts; with the help of art he creates a compromising yet acceptable scenario to himself.

139. *Nature* is vulgar from the perspective of culture; hence the real job of art lies in expressing the vulgar in socially acceptable forms.

140. If all other things are kept constant, then the purported notion of *morality* lies only in genes.

141. *Beauty* exists in the genes of an individual, and hence is known as a *subjective* quality. But a *group-living* in the past would have promoted the same sense of beauty among many individuals and that should have been assimilated into their genes gradually and sustained for many generations making it an *objective* quality of experience. However from an individual's perspective his own sense of beauty largely lies dormant within him and it manifests only when he meets the appropriate external circumstances.

142. For an adult man, the beauty of the mountains, grasslands, lakes, man-made mansions and palaces all lack the rigour of a *woman's face* he has already met or lying dormant in his genes. A man understands the sublimes of beauty only from the face of a woman; the beauty of a woman he liked is actually a complex process not fully understandable to him. The beauty already exists within him as a template. The beauty is not created and hence no one knows what is beauty to him until his in-built templates is invoked by something external to him. In this case a woman's face invokes his template of beauty and that is felt as desire.

A man's *desire* shows him absolutely clearly that nothing is more beautiful than the face of the women he likes. Here a big question, why he likes a particular woman so strongly, remains in the background unanswered. The answer can be derived from 'hate.' This is because 'hate' is more understandable than 'desire'. In practical world, a man loves beauty because of the causes far beyond his control but 'hates' the same beauty with few yet weak reasoning. *Thousands of genes and the biological imperatives of evolution come together and manifest as desire but a hate is decided only by decrepit and shallow feelings of mind. A man desires without knowing the causes but hates with his own known reason. A man is more conscious of his dislike than his likes!*

143. Not only today, even for many centuries from today, a *man* has to *naturally* depend upon *women;* only to divert from this hard, 'natural' fact men would nourish a culture in some form or the other. A man, consciously or unconsciously, always tries to make up his natural disadvantage with the help of culture and religion. It is men who originally created and sustained culture for their own benefit. This *culture* is a conscious blend of wealth, religion, reason and above all the God created by men to manage women; *as such without creating confusion a man can never win a woman!*

144. A *woman*, under normal lighting conditions, is more beautiful at a distance of about 8 metres. It is at this distance that what a man intends to observe is enhanced and what he does not is diminished!

145. E*very* man, at least at any one point of time in his life, thinks he is more competent, more useful, brave,

intelligent and beautiful than the others around him. However ridiculous this may seem to others or to himself at some other point of time, this *single* important *mental event* often decides his future unequivocally. This has a terrible impact, good or bad, on the rest of his life!

146. A man as part of a society is more cunning than if he had been an individual; the transformation from an individual to society is actually a transition from *fear* to *cunningness*; it is such an attitude of cunningness that ultimately leads to a *government*! After becoming a member of society, a man is under certain responsibility to perform; but each man as a member of a society, *mostly due to his inherent nature*, tacitly wants to be irresponsible. Nature dictates that such aversion towards responsibility can vary from person to person. But *each man due to tact and cunningness expects the other men to do what he does not intend to do; that sows the seeds of the inevitable necessity, called a government*. When the members of society increase in number, the only *reasonable arrangement* possible at such a large scale to accommodate the sum total of all cunningness turned out to be the *government*! It is a transition from *cunningness* to *reason*. Hence, from an *individual* to *society* to *government* is actually a transition from 'fear' to 'cunningness' to 'reason'.

147. A *woman* understands a man better than a *man* understands a woman! Man's roundabout ways and behaviour makes the situation easier for the generally intuitive women to quickly understand men. A man tries to understand women more through imagination than any realistic route; the idealistic and imaginary method adopted by most men is not suitable to capture a

woman's mind except in certain rare circumstances that are not known to both man and woman. Interestingly a woman does not want to understand herself and leaves that unwanted job to a man! Finally, a woman is neither understood by a man nor by the woman herself. Now, *it is a fact that a woman is the least understood of human reason yet most familiar creation of nature!* This simple fact has far-reaching implications on all of the man-woman relationships in any society across the world.

148. Whatever being or entity is justified in the name of *religion* is not intended to be unjustified; that is the tacit stand of all religious minded people who ensured the survival of various religions through the ages.

149. *Dreams* are first hand evidence that repeatedly prove that man is not the owner of his mind; to what extent a man understood the dreams is enough to show him how difficult and blind nature is itself.

150. There is no *cause and effect* but for a man sitting out there and tampering with nature; a cause and effect is a clear misunderstanding caused by man to himself due to his own conscious existence.

151. *Great men* are always *bad* and *great women* are always *mad*. Practically, the latter is an advanced form of the former! Bad is reversible and the mad is almost irreversible! Again between the two, the bad one is more conscious of his action than the mad one. Mad is badly unconscious and bad is madly conscious!

152. *Evolution* is a perpetual compromise between yesterday's decision and today's reality. Since the process involves *two* incidents and hence *time*. But nature has no time.

Time is a creation of man and hence evolution itself exists only for man. Nature never evolves but it seems so only for a man. Evolution is a man's most convincing way of looking back at nature to satisfy his senses and also be indifferent to his mind!

153. What a *man* can follow becomes his *culture* and whatever he cannot have has been made into culture for *other men!*

154. One end of human *consciousness* is nature and the other end is god! The one end is consciously unconscious and the other end is unconsciously conscious again only for consciousness. Human intelligence, tact, ignorance and any other kind of rational or irrational acts only try to justify or reconcile these two facts.

155. *Accident* gives birth to *design*; design exists within accident sometimes explicitly and at some other times inherently. Design is constructed by living beings at some corner of the accident. Local conditions accidentally create a design and handover to living things; in other words design is the way living things identify themselves within their surroundings, while an accident always exists at the background.

156. *Love* and *affection*: there is a *limit* up to which reason can direct a human mind, beyond which nature takes over; love happens above this limit and affection below it.

157. Greatest power, highest knowledge, and any other positive qualities or status of men and women are much less worth compared to *virtue*. *Virtue gives what a mind really longs for; the virtue is* understandable to anybody who has *patience* and has an ability to keep *quiet*. Virtue is not really taught by others; if so it would have been

possible to create numerous men of virtue every year but this never happens in real world. But what is virtue is known to the calm, clear and quiet mind. Hence, to keep quiet is the best of all possible qualities for both men and women in a society which came into existence to account for inherent cunningness in each individual. *Society is a mountain of cunningness under a snow cover of reason; the snow often melts only to reveal the mountain.* By *talking*, one can convince the other, but he cannot convince himself unless he keeps quiet.

158. The fact an apple exists here points also to another fact that 'the same apple does not exist' at some other place. The same applies to god also; otherwise it is totally impossible to account for the existence of different religions and belief systems; men are different and hence god. *Men can never become the same because nature would not allow them to be the same*. Hence religions have to be many in number with similar kinds of belief systems; within a religion individuals are different and have to be so and hence god varies from individual to individual; one has to only look at the behaviour of individuals to ascertain this fact. The *belief system is only a major frame work created by men as a member of society but individuals within them are answerable also to nature! Hence the nature of god varies to suit the nature of the individual mind.*

159. Whatever *exists* does not really exist; whatever does not exist already exists. A mind is capable disproving whatever is in existence and brings into existence what it does not intend to prove! A man accepts and lives with such contradictions, if not intimidating facts. This is

because the very of idea *existence* is nothing more than a mere acceptance by the human *mind*.

160. Really, there is no *free will* or *choice*. Freedom and choice are illusions created only due a man's understanding of local events and decisions made in connection to them. But the larger picture tells a different story. The first *truth* about our own existence is that men are never free; they have been *connected* in all conceivable directions. The connections when understood partially become *relations* which is the kernel of all sciences. All the time men try to understand the *relations* between the things with the help of senses and declare as if the things are fully understood. Free will is like relations while the fate is ingrained in connections. The free will is a conscious attempt made in *time* within the larger *fate* that exists behind the scene. When a tiny part of fate is felt in time it is claimed to be free will. *When a man is not free, where will the free will come from; a conscious man can have will but never free will.*

161. There exists a lot of purpose in life at an individual level. But life's purpose tends to diminish as the scale changes towards larger and larger or smaller and smaller from the present. This is the reason why a man gets confused when he compares the happenings at a larger level with his own individual actions with a purpose. In other words the world at large may seem random but at his individual level it would seem to have a purpose. The problem here is that his individual level happenings are more regular, whether good or bad it seems to be certain and deterministic or predictable but all from his own perspective only; this *local* and controlled mind set has an adequate resolution to understand and deal with the

environments in and around him; but if he looks at the world at large the elements of purpose cannot be seen. Again, even if he assumes his individual purposes at the local level are correct, he has to logically be ready to accommodate many similar purposes at the world at large and hence he has to necessarily accept a chaotic world of random events at a larger level; the same would happen if he proceeds from the local to the still micro level. *The purpose vanishes as the scale changes but this again is only from a human perspective.*

162. As society progress a man's source of *fear* starts shifting. For primitive men the source of fear was the very *nature* itself; the natural forces like storm, sun, volcano etc., threatened him. When his mind progressed further and he began to live in a better organized society, the other *fellow men* became the source of fear. In the next stage of development, a man becomes highly developed with individual freedom as his natural right, he fears for himself; his *freedom* seems to be threatening. He is not able to manage himself despite having everything he is expected to have to meet the standards of the societal environment where he lives; but now he is afraid of his own *self*. Hence he again goes back to the *nature* and *fellow men* to manage himself. A man goes on tour to see nature and arranges parties and festivals only to manage or escape from his own *freedom*. He wants to fix his mind on something other than itself. He does a thousand other things only because he fails to do the *one* most important thing, that is: to *befriend his own self*.

163. Life is actually a man's continuous search for *reference*. The futile search never really gives him any other reference

but finally falls back to him as a reference. Ultimately there is no wonder or worthy reference, beyond him.

164. A statement that everything is *changing* every time has no meaning unless there is *something* that *never changes*, however stupid the idea of the something may be.

165. A man likes someone because of his *reason*, but he loves some other because of his *nature*.

166. Reason as an accident should have first occurred in *men* only and its very first achievement should have been in the possession of *women*!

167. Man being a social animal, most often the *worrying* becomes the first and easiest thing. The predominant source of such worry is more of cultural and less natural. Man understands '*culture*' more easily than his own '*nature*'. This makes him incapable of a balancing act between the culture and nature. No doubt culture is the basic controlling mechanism against the rude and often crude nature. But, no effective control is possible without understanding nature itself hence the 'worrying'.

168. Human *life*, is it a *choice* or *design? From* day to day perspectives the '*choice*' becomes clear to our mind. It does not mean that there is no element of 'design'. This is because, behind all our actions, there is *a desire* the source of which is *not* clearly known to us. The desire is actually *innate*, but we actively promote the innate desire by superficially believing as if it is our intelligent choice. *Desire is not our choice but we wrongly understand it as our choice*; the width and depth of a desire lies elsewhere and only its tip is manifested within a living human being. The existence of such innate desire convinces us

that a choice is already made by some body, and hence the design!

169. *Democracy* and *capitalism* are an unholy combination. At least in theory, one is predominantly 'mental' and the other is 'material'. While the democracy aims at larger interest of society and the capitalism promotes individual interest; the first one is for *freedom* and the other is for *material*. In the combined situation, democracy ensures human freedom and the unfettered freedom is an evil to individuals' weak minds, the ones with only materialist ambitions. Evidently, *a weak mind always mixes both freedom and material wealth in the wrong way; the weak don't know the proportion of the blend that is beneficial to him. The consequence is that a man is in the hands of materials rather than it being the other way around; in simple terms democracy makes all* the *preparatory measures necessary for exploitation of society by one or more men.*

170. *Life* starts with *questions*. Since birth a man somehow becomes an expert in making up questions; his mind grows only with questions every day; but answering becomes very hard and sometimes impossible even for great intellectuals, particularly if the questions pertain to the fundamental issues like time and space etc. Even great minds immediately search for some kind of answers and are subsequently concerned about the 'correctness' of *answers*! Here the concerned answering minds act in a routine way by granting validity to such questions; when the mind toils so much to answer all such questions, it forgets to question the question itself, which is whether all of these questions themselves are valid or not. I sincerely

think due to the brief reasons stated below that certain questions involving *time*, *space*, *mass*, *creation* and so on are local and *invalid* at a much larger scale and hence trying to find answers for them cannot be anything but only the passing of some time.

A major fault in the *common way of thinking is that* the *human mind automatically tries to believe the ideas and concepts that are relevant and useful at a local level are also useful and applicable in the same way at a global level.* For instance, *size*, *shape* and *time* are *concepts* created only based on a man's local sensual experience and requirements but the same is taken for granted at the level of the *universe*. These local sense-based concepts are relevant mainly for purposes like *survival* and locomotion and to that extent only they are strictly valid. Once these concepts are extended beyond the immediate surroundings to the level of an assumed universe, where the senses have no capacity or resolution and also where the natural necessity for survival does not exist, these concepts become totally irrelevant.

When we start applying theses concepts from a local level and proceed towards the global level the same concepts get *distorted 'on the way through'* and totally vanish at the level of the universe. There arises a question concerning how to understand this universe without these *abstract* concepts. There are two possibilities: one is to throw away these concepts; the other is to throw away the idea of universe itself. These *simple* and *local* concepts, notwithstanding local usefulness, have deceived us for centuries and cannot aid us in understanding the universe. Again there arises a problem, without these concepts the mind itself cannot function!

A human mind after producing these three abstract ideas with the help of senses has already exhausted its limit. All these three concepts have been created by something, in this instance by the mind, by assuming that the very mind itself exists outside of the things to which these concepts are applicable; the very such assumption is not feasible in case of the mind versus the *universe!* After all nothing can exist outside the universe to apply these concepts. As such the mind is ultimately left alone without any concept to define the universe; this leads to a bizarre conclusion *that whatever exists, however big or small it may be, is only local and there is nothing called universe but for the mindless projection of a mind!*

171. One reason why culture is more biased towards *men* than *women* can be answered by taking a cue from nature itself. We know that *nature* and *culture* are often found standing up against each other. Any sensible men of experience would quickly understand that women are more *natural* than men. Women are natural because they are sincere to their own feelings. This makes women capable of surviving adverse circumstances where most average men would perish. Men understood long back that women can live without men, due to their natural advantage; having understood this, men created culture with their might and brute power and asked women to follow it. Therefore with the help of culture, men tried to balance the situation if not reverse. Despite all these attempts, still a man is only an extension of women and the reverse cannot be true!

172. Even today *religion* is still mental and but *rituals* have become business propositions; and this is thanks to the modern priests, the cunning dupes who accumulate

wealth in the name of spiritualism! Yesterday men of religion intended to detach material from men and today men do the reverse.

173. *Good men* will always fight with themselves; they continuously create their own mental contradictions that finally turned out to be their wisdom!

174. *Intelligence* and *stupidity* have an equal chance of taking a man to divinity! This is because *nature* does not make any distinction.

175. A man's *own strength* is not known to him until a patient listening to his own inner voice or an accidental encounter that most likely happens in his routine life.

176. Men celebrate any unexpected good as *luck* but any unexpected bad as *fate*. Again both are unexpected, but real life exists somewhere in between them.

177. Technically speaking *gravity* is an effect; it can be felt because it affects others but cannot be detected by experiment. Therefore gravity is not a positive entity in the sense to be captured by any instrument. The speed and damages of *wind* can be measured but no one can detect the very wind itself but only the air molecules; here, the cause of wind is known as the air molecules but not the wind itself, yet the effect of wind is felt. The same thing happens in case of God. Hence, god is an effect! The cause of god is human mind, akin to the air molecules.

178. There is nothing called *physical* separation between two things at any level. After all, in between any two externally existing things the senses neither have a jurisdiction nor do they have competency.

179. *Women* say directly what they do not like and indirectly what they like. A man without knowing this often takes the first one more seriously than the second one only to be wrong at both occasions.

180. *Women*: in the day to day world it is often true that an average woman is very unpredictable, even by a man of intelligence; this is because the woman is *natural* while the man uses reason; again when a man is natural the woman becomes predictable. They cross paths but alas only for a brief period.

181. *Women* align with either nature or culture effortlessly. *Men* also intend to do the same, but do so with difficulty. The probable reason for this may be: while women make their necessities coincide with nature, men try to look at the man-made circumstances, particularly the social considerations, to arrive at a decision. Hence women generally take faster decisions than men.

182. *Women* are weak, but only up to a limit. *Men* are strong, again only up to a limit. In real life both the limits rarely coincide. Marriage is one such point of coincidence!

183. It is for men: in day to day life, if a woman doesn't want something she actually wants it. Again, if she wants, then she certainly wants it!

184. A beautiful *woman* does not know how to cross a road.

185. *Education* affects *women* and *men* distinctly: it is *able* to make women manifest their inner nature better than men. Again it is not uncommon for men to consciously, if not proactively, go against the authority of education to hide their own nature.

186. *Good* and *bad* exist at same place, at same time and in the same thing or person. If a man finds an angel in a *woman*, he need not search elsewhere for a ghost. But the man either by accident or by intelligence can invoke in women only one of the two at a time.

187. It is a speculation on the future of the relationship between *men-women*: the world will be predominantly polyandrous 200 years from now. The technology and the associated *specializations* would have irreversibly distorted the men both mentally and physically; evolution would have played its role very well and the *consciousness* of men would have been made them unconscious about *nature*. But women would have largely escaped from such distortion and the onslaught of specialization and would have been able stay closer to nature! Thus women would have gained more mental control and independence to look after life and events rather than the men.

188. A man is forced to act first then justify it subsequently. His reason is conscious of what is being justified but unconscious of who forced it. The *fate* is stored in the unconscious region.

189. There is no *life*, if a man is not able to justify his own existence at least with a story.

190. Intelligent men never do a *business*; only a fool kills his own beautiful instincts for the sake of the word *profit*. While no one can ignore the fact that *this word* ensures the survival of numerous human beings in any social set-up, it is the very same word that distorts a man's mind, cripples his reason and destroys his conscience only to silently commit unimaginable cruelties and sins specific

only to human beings; the mind, reason and conscience all are overpowered by the word *profit* only to make a human as inhuman.

191. *Hope* and *trust* are excellent parameters to test an individual's patience and genuine relationship respectively; while hope works wonders for an individual, the trust does the same for a relationship.

192. A *business* fails when motive becomes more important than the *trust*.

193. The greatest defect of *democracy* is that it treats everybody as equal while actually they are not so. The result is while the *law* tries to treat every subject equal, the subjects themselves want to create in equalities! This is because equality creates distaste in human sensibilities; hence often it becomes a *necessity* to create inequalities to meet the practical requirements; democracy disturbs the natural compatibility while individuals struggle to restore it. This way in an actual democracy the laws of human reason are occasionally implemented while the *nature takes care of the practical affairs of individuals*.

194. Every *human action* has a history. If anyone finds it out, that would become the justification for the same action.

195. *Art* is the daughter of an *instinct*. Hence it is as good or as bad as the instinct behind it.

196. The jurisdiction of the *mind* is more than *man* and of God is less than the mind. God is a mentor of man and is a son of the mind.

197. *Art* neither has a *reason* nor an *intuition*. If an art cannot spoil a man, nobody in the world can do it to him.

198. Nature 'hands over' a part of itself as an *instinct* to a man and when the man takes over, the instinct gets modified as his intention. This way a man's jurisdiction starts with his *intention*. Hence in all human activities an *idea* is more important than *work*; *intention* is more important than the idea.

199. *Power* is man's natural instinct. If he blends a bit of trick and shame it turns out to be *politics*!

200. The *senses* carve out a tiny part of the world and declare it as material things. Since the *mind* is already connected with a large network of both visible and invisible senses, it finally belittles the claims of human senses.

201. By *enlightenment*, a man is finally duped by his own *mind*! The mind attached to a man is small and evolves along with the brain. But the real mind is enormous and extends beyond man. The *larger mind* tries to teach him as long as he is capable and ready to receive instructions; in this process the *smaller mind* keeps expanding. When he becomes tired of receiving lessons it cannot expand itself, instead it starts preaching itself; but it is actually duping, often once for all. An ordinary man becomes tired quickly hence he is duped by a smaller portion of his small mind. But a sage has large mind due to regular practice and hence he does not become tired easily, yet he is duped by a larger portion of his large mind!

202. *The Mind* and the *body* are two of the most 'miss-fit' things always fitted together by *nature* and offered as a permanent gift to human beings for possessing *reason*!

203. *Man* and *nature*: at any instance a sum total of my feelings is my nature and his feelings is his nature. Nature reflects

on man, again man reflects on nature. It is a subjective and two-way process. As such there in no nature waiting 'out' *there* for human interpretation, independent of his own nature! *Reason* is a one way thinking; hence the world is not always amenable to the reason. *Reason* finds only a foot path in the forest; it does not show the forest itself.

204. If human thinking and hence *intentions* are not stored outside the human physical realms, then the very existence of *religions* is not feasible.

205. All *ambitious minds* want to create only one thing to enhance its all kind of *intentions*, *expectations* and *motives*: that one thing is God. All *fearful minds* want to believe only in one thing for its *survival*: again that one thing turned out to be a God.

206. A faith or *belief system* is a necessary consequence of the nature of the mind. The wandering nature of the mind creates its own little yet stable system as some kind of safety valve to rely on; this way a *belief or faith becomes a basic and necessary element for the very functioning of any mind.* Nobody is beyond such kind of belief: if someone cannot believe in God but only in reason, he still believes in something because he has a mind and it has to necessarily function; hence a *belief* becomes the starting point for any mind to function. All other interpretations of the world have its origins only in that belief!

207. *Arrogance*: by being arrogant a man only kills a portion of his own mind.

208. Apart from the original fear, a human society became possible and sustainable due to the differences in human

capabilities, both *mental and physical. Similarly if animals form society they also should have differences in their instincts; if all animals are endowed with the same nature of instinct they cannot have a society!*

209. *Art* begins when a mind fancies an *improved* version of nature. But such enriched images and interpretations of the things never really satisfy the mind that started it. Instead, subsequently the art takes the mind from the ground realities of world only to make it more vulnerable by blocking *reason* and *intuition*, the guiding spirits of any matured human beings. Art makes the susceptible mind fall for something less real, the art itself!

210. *Man* and *his mind*: a man's mind is more the man! The *man* is like a tip of the iceberg but the iceberg itself is his *mind*. The total size of the iceberg decides how much of it is to be visible above the water's surface as a 'man'. The surrounding water and the sky above in the form of mighty *nature* decide the very size of the iceberg itself. Hence, man is an extension of his mind and the mind is a bridge connecting man and nature.

211. *Politics* works on a principle that an idiot who knows more idiots is an intelligent! In other words the majority don't know the one also as an idiot.

212. *Weak men* don't like truth, but expect what they like it to be true.

213. Scientifically, it is possible to connect a man's anger of today to a mental setting of his forefathers a million years back. This fact makes the man and hence the world around him as a continuous entity.

214. A *man* who thinks all his thinking processes originate within him is stupid. The *brain* is a two way antenna that receives signals from one side known to us as *instinct* and emits signals on the other side as *intentions*. A man is often conscious of both incoming and outgoing signals without being able to control them. Therefore, a *man himself is created and came in to existence out of those processes of the reception and emission of signal without fully knowing the closed loop formed by the both signals!*

215. Originally nature threatened men and hence the God, but today *god* is necessary to protect men from *materialism* since materials threaten men more than the nature. Again if the so called spiritualists of today do not intend to posses materials they don't need God! While the well known wisdom of spiritualism is detachment, how can any state allow attachment of materials by *modern sages* in the name of spiritual practice, unless the state is stupid?

216. If *accidents* happen in very large numbers, in the process the *design* becomes an automatic possibility at some corners of those numerous accidents. In reality, accident and design are not two independently existing things; *accident and design are inseparable*. Both actually exist as one and the same thing understood differently. The human mind has a filter within itself; when it seeks to look at order it filters disorder, when it looks for disorder it filters the order resulting either in accident or design!

217. *Nature at any local level* is neither efficient nor perfect, but is *effective*. The effectiveness necessarily involves some kind of imperfection. This imperfection is a prerequisite for nature to be dynamic!

218. *Truth* need not necessarily exist as *physical* events but can very well be a *mental* process. Again, the latter can be as useful or useless as the former!

219. *Life* is like a wide river course. Assume that one man travels along the banks of the river and another man on the water course itself without being able to see the banks. The man on the bank is exposed to various topographical features all along the river bank and hence able relate the nature of water flow to the surrounding physical features. As such he is able to *experiment* with the river banks and watercourse.

But another man travelling along the water course has no possibility of looking around at any of the geographical features because the river is very wide and sees only water everywhere. Therefore he *experiences* what the nature of flowing water offers him, either the turbulence or tranquillity, his mind interprets the world accordingly.

The one on the bank has ample opportunities to explain the nature of the water flow based on the physical features on which the water flows from its youthful stage of rapids and falls to its matured stage of calm meanders; for this man the senses are *active* and immensely useful to satisfy his curious mind. The other man on the water course only undergoes varied experiences without any feasibility for experimenting and hence depends only on his *mind* for explanation of what he experiences; for this man the senses only act like *passive* partners to the mind.

Ultimately the parallel we draw here is that *science* is like the man who treads on the banks, and *religion* is like the other man on the water course!

220. In human life *accident* and *design* work alongside one another; for good men *happiness* comes out of design and *misery* is due to accident; for bad people the reverse happens!

221. *Mind* and *nature* are different ways of misunderstanding the same thing!

222. The *madness* of a man has no limit until another man, at least with slightly more madness, shows him the limit! It is strange that everything has a *limit* in the practical world except the human *madness*, the worst kind of directionless intelligence!

223. *Perception* is not the limit of nature. There is a limit up to which the senses perceive nature as being sensible objects; not able to perceive beyond this limit does not mean that *nature* does not exist.

224. *Uncertainty* is proportional to *certainty;* thus the religion and science would grow in proportion to each other. The constant of proportionality is the 'nature of human mind' that changes constantly!

225. Perception cheats in the name of *reason* and belief cheats in the name of *religion*. There is no escape, since the perception only created the reason and belief only created the religion! Hence a man is already hitched to one of these pursuits, and ends up just glorifying the one that suits him.

226. *Spiritualism* cannot be preached to others without making it, more often than not, a business; therefore a man who preaches to himself is a real *sage*. In politics, the follower makes a leader stupid; in religion the followers make the preacher a *dupe*. If any one finds an exception, then he

is a good follower! *Men never change but only methods change.*

227. On *normal human mind*: intentions and beliefs inescapably occupy certain portion of mind resulting religion. Simultaneously the mind and senses together collect the events, facts and figures giving birth to reason.

228. A *ruler of a state* needs a heart as large as the state if not bigger. Unquestionably the well being of the state's subjects depends on how big the heart of the ruler is. The brain too is important but can be hired!

229. Beware of a *sage;* nobody serves the society by killing his own instinct and there is no necessity from any other side but for nature's incapacitation.

230. In the real world, *power* often becomes compensation for stupidity.

231. When *truth* exists nearby, a weak mind may evade it. The weak and fearful mind intends to go to such a distance that it can only have a faint look or no look at all. Only for those it becomes hard to get rid of fear, the truth exists at a far way distance.

232. A stupid person's action is justified by *instinct* while the action by an intelligent is justified by *reason*!

233. *Reality* is a product of four cooks: the mind, the senses, the object and its environment. But of all, *mind* is the master cook.

234. This is an old issue, *on perception*: it is *a world in-itself. There is an organic continuity among what perceives, what is perceived as material things and its surroundings*: this is the basic frame work of *physical existence* from a human

perspective that necessarily involves all of the senses and the mind. When we go further into what constitutes the *material things*, the same vanishes seamlessly with its surroundings. The human senses chisel out material objects out of the continuous surroundings; sometimes the mind uses as many as five chisels, the five senses, at one time to carve out a 'material thing'.

The opaqueness, physical extent, colour are combined result due to the *coalescence* of *mind* and its *senses* on one side, the *material things* and its *surroundings* on the other; interestingly none of them have a valid individual existence! The colour perceived is neither in mind nor in material things alone; the colour derives its existence from each and every one of these. As such the colour as a property has *four* owners: the mind, senses, material thing and surroundings. It is the result of the totality of circumstances. Here, neither the argument that the object of perception is purely mental nor the argument that it exists out there only as an objective material thing is untenable. *During perception there cannot exist two distinct entities one belonging to the mental and the other only to the material.* Accordingly the *mind, senses, material thing* together with the *surroundings* produce a fifth one, the *colour*: there exists an organic continuity among all the four before production of the colour. Therefore the origin of the colour has to be necessarily traced back to all the four.

Hence perception is a subjective phenomenon with respect to all the four: all the four *coalesce* into one and make this colour a possibility. Therefore the colour cannot exist independently even if *any one* of these four is absent. However, all are valid only from a human perspective!

235. *Art* works to satisfy the instinct and the *science* works to satisfy reason.

236. *Men* originally acquired power, wealth and status with an intention *to possess* women. Hence the subsequent struggle among men became natural consequences of that intention. Today women try to acquire the *same* but *to be free* from men and hence it did not create similar struggles among women!

237. *Politicians* cannot change *politics* due to the fact that they enter politics only after becoming politicians! *A fish cannot bail the water out*, however someone outside the water can.

238. *Truth* is a bare fact until human beings interpret it as good and bad. Each society uses its *own scales of judgment* of which one side is *good* and the other side is *bad*. As such the truth has no place in the world of good and bad. However, the left over traces of truth manage to exist at the thin border between the good and bad. This way the *truth* exists at the junction between good and bad.

239. *Democracy* is a sin, not even an acceptable sin but rather an accepted sin. *Democracy is born and brought up as everyone intends to practice their own possible deceit at sometime or the other*. The *equality* in democracy is essentially deceitful and induces exploitation. The beauty and realism inevitably happen in the natural gradation of material things and events relating them. Democracy and the associated false freedom lead to the wrong mixing of the right things. This way democracy always leads to

widen the inequality in accepted ways; the promises of freedom and equality seduce men to accept it and the *cunning of reason* works day and night to justify it.

Further, democracy helps men define and practice equality and freedom without consulting nature. In democracy the freedom and equality is being applied to people as if they are mentally and physically same; the people are bodily present today but mentally and physiologically each one lives in different time periods! Therefore applying democracy, with equality and freedom, to such human stock only bodes ill and spreads indiscipline. *Democracy often creates intelligent slaves and free idiots!*

240. Perversion is a sleeping monster; *art* is a fawning mistress. *Art* serves the perversion that is deep and often dormant within a man.

241. Human life is essentially the story of a *small mind* attached to man longing to meet and understand, the *larger mind* attached to nature. While both are actually continuous the actions of senses and reason create an apparent discontinuity between them. Therefore to make the man's life significant and meaningful his small mind accepts the onus of responsibility to overcome this divide with an intention of finding solace in the large mind!

242. Reason does the great job of the *timing*: when a man has to be a man and when he has to be an animal!

243. *Art* is buried deeply inside human beings and therefore it should have been the language of communications between animals, the precursor to human beings. In other words, by *art* an animal moves closer to man and a man moves closer to animals!

244. I belong to the category of men who believe that *everything* is connected with every other thing. While extending this argument I do not believe the isolated one-way arguments either by science or by religion. *Everything* is created by *mind* is wonderful; but then arises the logical question of who created the mind. *The answer is that the mind itself is created by the same everything! Obviously this fact only makes one ponder the wonder of all possible wonders, the mind.* This circular way of understanding the nature of mind is inescapable since it is always the mind that has to either create or accept or ratify something as a wonder. The mind sits over the judgment on its own creation; this way the mind becomes the mother of all wonders! However, stupid or intelligent a mind may be, there is no wonder waiting outside until the mind accepts it so.

245. Ashrams: if women stop going to *ashrams, which is* a highly unlikely situation, fifty percent of them will be shut down. If states stop permission and abolish the acceptance of donations, the remaining forty nine percent would vanish; but the world is still left with that one percent of sacredness!

246. *Instinct* ensures that animals have society. *Reason* ensures society has animals.

247. If the body works for the sake of mind it is *love; if* the mind works for the sake of the body it is *lust*!

248. The development of the *mind* passes through several stages: *sport*, *art*, *reason* and finally to *intuition*. *Sport* is largely physical, more of a skill than imagination and hence nearer to nature. *Art* is bit more of a manifestation of instinct and imagination than sport however it doesn't

contain the reason within it; hence the art is vulnerable to the reason of others or it has to depend on the reason and intuition of others for its protection. *Reason* plays all games till it surrenders to intuition. *Intuition* is an inner mental strength and is not bothered about individuals and individual events but the relation between minds and mind and nature and subsequent experiences that impacts human beings.

249. Certainly, *arrogance* is not bravery. It works well in presence of the *weak* and *innocent* and more importantly with *cunning* people. These *three* always depend on others either due to their very nature or for their survival. While the first two are naturally understandable, third one has been promoted due to the *stupidity* always associated with arrogance. History shows, it always becomes easy for cunning men to work with arrogant and yet stupid man! The very nature of arrogance is to overlook the intelligence of others and hence this unintentionally paves the way for cunning men to get closer to it. *No one can ever be able to find an arrogant man or woman not surrounded either by idiots or by cunning people*; if someone finds an intelligent man as arrogant then the former is idiot enough to enable the latter to hide more than what he reveals. Arrogance is a tactical way of escaping from intelligence only to create a false sense of security. Arrogance is surrounded by dupes and hence the insecurity is inherent in it.

250. Throughout history eccentric men were frequently and very conveniently misunderstood as intelligent. This is because the *idiots do not have the qualification to become eccentric*!

251. *Science* begins with matter and ends with the *mind*. *Religion* started with the mind and ends with *matter*. The difference exists only in the starting point; both declare the starting point as the *cause* and the end as *effect*! It is obvious that if both the paths overlap they have to be certainly a meeting point; that *one point* will show the stupidity of 'human reason' and its weakness dividing the nature into the two distinct interpretations and sustaining the same with numerous justifications, that too differently at different times!

252. Even scientifically the *evolution* is a continuous process of *creation*. Hence creation is already a part of the natural process of evolution. Therefore one need not worry about the question pertaining to creation but rather focus on *who* creates! The human mind that tries to answer questions pertaining to '*who creates*' *by* adopting an objective or a scientific route makes the answers either suit its individual mental capability or mental preferences. If that mind is under the direction of reason, then the creation has to be seen from the perspective of reason. Since the *reason* always looks from *outer* world to inner nature of things, it seems as if the *nature* does the job of creation. However, if the same mind depends on faith or some kind of *religion*, its perspective is from *inner* human nature to outer, there arises the *purpose* and as such the *God* creates the world. *Reason is indifferent to the purpose that takes place at individual levels for its own reasons. Religion is indifferent to the chaos that happens on a much larger scale again for its own reasons!* This way the very world is at the grace of the state of individual human mind.

253. *God* helps a man subject to the limit that he himself imposes on God!

254. *Infinity* is the confluence of the smallest and the largest. Therefore *infinity* and *zero* are one and same, hence the world is circuitous!

255. By love, *nature* evaporates the strength of human *reason* to assert its supremacy. The poor reason is left alone only to reappear as a supporter!

256. *Spiritualism* is so individualistic that even an addition of one more man makes it a *business*, if not an *exploitation*.

257. A man's *actions* of today depend more on what he doesn't know than what he knows very well!

258. *Art* is as real as a mirage and hence works well at a distance.

259. *Desire* is the most complex of all decisions without involving a man; behind a man's desire there exists a million variables. The poor man is left alone only to implement it.

260. When a man is worried and desires of banking on his *physical strength* he should remember about the existence of animals!

261. A good *relationship* involves the satisfaction of both *instinct* and *reason*!

262. *Ignorance* has two sides: to love and to hate. *Intelligence* has only one side: to keep quiet.

263. *Consciousness* is subjective to the extent that each brain is unique in construction. Therefore, each man is an idiot in a unique way. Human beings are by and large idiots of different levels and types. Science in trying to project *objectivity* intends to make us only '*one type*' of idiots!

264. *Science* is nothing but a broken *religion*!

265. *Consciousness* is only a small part of the mind accessible to man, say his brain. But it acts as a connection between a man and the *mind* in a unique and mystical way.

266. A belief that one *causes* another is the starting point of all subsequent forms of stupidities.

267. *History* is a written distortion of facts; but for the distortion it would only show how bad real human beings are when they look at themselves. History not only distorts but exaggerates on either way. *History is born when we do not indent to appreciate our real nature.*

268. If the bulk of men are not *idiots* the kingdoms of yesterday and *democracy* of today would not have been feasible.

269. *Art* is a big trap; it promises an *idealism* superior to the common man's but its *realism* is much worse than that of the average man.

270. *Reason* has no universal basis. Practical world shows, even the ignorant and idiots can have enough reasoning powers, although this may be only to their own peril, to seriously believe that the fraudulent acts of most politicians as brave and socially significant ones and the funny traits of cunning modern priests as holy acts!

271. The appeal of *religion* lies in its usefulness for every occasion. It is a collection of *ready-made justifications* for human existence for most of the times and *exploitation* for rest of the times! It is *fun*, it is *solace* and it is also a *sin*.

272. Being either *good* or *bad* is a continuous struggle!

273. Everything can be reduced to the *mind* and the mind cannot be reduced further!

274. The only difference between any two things of this phenomenal world, either living or non-living, is in the *time*.

275. The statements '*mind* makes everything' and '*everything* makes the mind' is indistinguishable; both are equally valid at all the times. Neither the experience nor the logic would be of any help to prove which is wrong and which is right.

276. It is obvious that hell or heaven is only a state of mind. A man whose mind is in the state of *concentration* is already in heaven. All other times his mind is either in hell or on the way to it.

277. *On prudence*: a polite man is more dangerous than an angry man.

278. Despite the progress of human civilization, still all human actions, including *reason*, are basically instinctive in nature. Reason *is never an independent authority.*

279. A lioness hunts and waits for lion to eat the prey first. The lion demarcates its territory and protects it from other lions. I do not want to attribute these behaviours to instinct alone and claim that animals do not have *reason*. Animals do have reason like human beings; but the difference is that they never overdo it, justify or explain actions!

280. It is not always *prudent* to interpret all human actions as being either *rational* or *irrational* and denigrates the latter; beneath all these human actions there exists a life preserving intent.

281. The *mind* and *reason* of both animals and human beings need not necessarily be within their physical body; they

can be anywhere, either inside or outside or both, it all depends on the nature of the living being's interaction with the world bodily external to it. Further, subject to its constitution the physical body has a capacity to tap the mind available everywhere.

282. *Reason* is the discretionary power of man. This residual power handed over to a man in the process of evolution of instinct is often wrongly understood as being a distinct faculty of the mind. *Reason* is not a unique attribute of human beings, animals do have some reason but not fully manifested. Reason is only an extension of the mighty instinct largely lying dormant inside all life forms. *Instinct is the unconscious director of human reason.*

283. Even ten thousand years down the line, the value of the word *morality* will survive; because only few would follow morality. Those few who follow would know the importance of it and the bulk of those who violate also would only increase the importance! It is strange, *any appreciation and regard for a 'norm' is derived more from those who breach it than those follow it!*

284. The *truth* is modified according to human nature and social living as being *good* and *evil*. Both the good and bad are socially relative and do not have any independent existence, yet they over shadow the existence of truth.

285. A *man* justifies today, because he does not know what tomorrow will be.

286. *Men* make their own simple minds complicated in the first-half of their lives, in the second half they try exactly the reverse, and often unsuccessfully. Most *women*, if not all, don't do this foolish job of creating distress today

for the sake of tomorrow, even if it promises a great advancement.

287. The nature of the *God* is decided by the mind along with local circumstances despite man's longing for something far external.

288. *Nature of life*: each living creature is controlled and guided by some forces, either visible or invisible, but always in association with it. That living being or animal together with the said forces constitute a world in itself. As such each and every animal, however small or big it may be, has its own world; the world that is *almost* unique to that *particular species* actually often overlap with the worlds specific to other species; while its own individual world seems to be in *order* to that animal and its species, the overlapping causes *disorder* among individual members of species. What happens is, with the help of instinct or reason an individual being is able to largely manage only its own world, but it is hardly aware of the happenings other worlds. Therefore, every living creature is being influenced, directed and handled by all other worlds that exist around it all the time, apart from its own world! *This frame work of a living being own world overlapping with the surrounding worlds becomes the cause of 'uncertainty of existence' of that individual living thing.* Hence, each living being feels *instinctively* threatened throughout their existence.

289. One cannot locate something that exists everywhere; that would lead to a situation in which what is *certain* becomes *uncertain*.

290. Man is nothing but his *mind*. The mind may have a thousand definitions again depending on the very mind

that defines it. I define *'mind as a sum of relationships that are known and also unknown'*. In the case of human beings the mind gradually came into existence by relating itself with others; it is a simultaneous process of its own awareness along with the awareness of all others that surrounds it, both visible and invisible. Therefore a *human mind* is not there prior to such awareness and only comes into existence along with *awareness*. But the awareness part is insignificantly small in comparison to its connections that it is not yet aware of and that makes a human mind strange and wonderful to itself.

291. *The nature of* the *mind* is not to be static. The mind and thoughts are constantly jumping, a *normal* mind jumps frequently to establish more and more relationships with others and itself; the others may be any animate or inanimate things. Once it establishes a relation, subsequently it repeats the same with the help of its memory as frequently as it desires. Hence a mind jumps aimlessly from one thing to another either actual or virtual. What is born in such an aimless process is the enormous and mighty young thing, called *reason*!

292. C*reation* itself is from disorder; order cannot create anything.

293. Any *idea* or *concept* may first start with a desire or passion or obsession or natural inclination depending on the individual's circumstances. During the initial stages, the idea or *concept* is completely under the control of the individual who created it but subsequently the concept grows in its importance and stature far beyond the man who created it. Soon such *concepts* get independence from him and exist on their own. But its independence

is only from the perspective of the creator, they are not absolute in the sense that they still depend on the individual who created it or on others who impart them with meaning, existence and utilization.

294. What one thinks matters, but what really matters is how strong and intensive the *thinking* itself is. It is the *intensity* of the thinking that creates the required chemical changes in him, leading to its originally intended consequences either good or bad!

295. A man exists in his *feelings*, an animal exists in its *instinct* and an object is in its *relation* with others.

296. *Reason* is the armour of a young man while the *intuition* is the same for a matured man.

297. *Abstraction* is definitely not real, but it is one of the greatest and most often inescapable tools that a human mind is accomplished to understand the *real*.

298. It is obvious that all *idiots* cannot become *powerful.* However, the easiest thing that any idiot can do is to become powerful. This is because power is a natural instinct, it comes naturally for everybody. But idiots are the first section of people who are deeply influenced, rather affected badly or often driven mad by power; *instinct impacts idiots first. Power involves the use of less of the human 'brain' than all other areas of human endowments like reason, discipline, morality and many other qualities that involve concern for others.*

299. The word '*I*' should actually mean what a man is *aware* of and how better his mind can *reflect* on it.

300. A man is not the owner of all the *words* he speaks. Often, he is only talking on behalf of his *genes* that already

took the decision on what he has to talk about; but who triggers the *gene* is unknowingly known as god!

301. *Religion is good but it is extremely difficult for those who preach to also be good!* In the practical world the latter is more important than former. Only in the sphere of religion, breaches are more than what is actually preached.

302. It is evident from history that all *religions* have been used as a form of social control and regulator of individual minds. But *strangely* the religions make human beings more *instinctive* and often let loose the control on *senses;* otherwise it is difficult to account for the existence of religious places as centres of human sensual relief if not exploitation of women. Mind becomes light and plain and that makes it easy for human beings to forget the sensual morality at religious places!

303. Scientifically *life* is nothing but an unfolding of frequencies.

304. There is nothing called *separate entities* in the world. It is worth it here to remember the existence of the *mind* and its *servants*!

305. *Evolution* is not an isolated event. The evolution is an unfolding of something that cannot happen without the participation of the things around, the near and far.

306. The one who behaves for the sake of others' perception is an *unfortunate man.*

307. *Women* are culturally less deviant than men. This is because *men* made the *culture* in that way. Culture has been made as a tool to control human instinct. However, for biological and survival reasons, men try to

selectively control women's instincts more than their own. Accordingly, men make the culture, definitely by trial and error, in such a way that it can be followed more by women and less by men. Again, interestingly men always used it *selectively*!

308. Out of all forms of governance, *democracy* involves a lot of comedy in the name of freedom. It is a consciously acceptable, if not a legal way of fooling one another; any democracy only projects *freedom* on one side to veil the *justice* on the other side.

309. *Intelligent* and *idiots* are not two different breeds of men. The former reached the destination earlier than the latter. The one took a straight route while the other is wasting the time in a circuitous route by meeting the power, status and money.

310. A man's *belief* will work certainly, but to a certain extent only! For more benefits he has to broaden or change the very belief itself.

311. The *mind* understands something, misunderstands 'some other things' and believes yet another thing. The mind is doubtful about its understanding and certain about its misunderstanding; hence the mind has to necessarily *believe* on 'something' that it neither understood nor misunderstood but yet to be understood. In short, the mind likes what it cannot understand or does not understand or does not want to understand! *Human mind has a strange tendency to go beyond understandable things and firmly believes in them only.*

312. *Life* may be often frustrating since *man* is not able understand it. But if at all he understands, it would be

much more frustrating! *'Nature' keeps most subtle secrets within itself for good reasons.*

313. *Freedom* fathers more and more *profane* and only little *sacred*, even that little is only claimed as so without proof.

314. An *individual's* action by itself has no meaning and 'value' if all others and its circumstances are excluded.

315. There is no principle or divine idea waiting there independent of a man's *mind*.

316. The *mind* starts with the senses and joins itself inseparably with physical world during the initials stages of its formation. Once these sense based judgments gradually becomes a substratum, the mind subsequently drops the senses to create another 'mental world' of superstructure on the substratum without the aid of senses. This *mental world* does not need senses anymore and mind is its own will to make modifications to suit its comfort and convenience; this way a mind thinks that it has abilities to eliminate the discrepancies and deficiencies of real world, dominated by senses. Finally a matured mind has two worlds, *physical* and *mental*, to accommodate itself and also avail benefits from the world that suits it.

317. The *mind* declares a real world illusionary only to adore his imaginary mental world as real. A mind that is able to make the real world as illusionary with certain parameters that have origin only in the resolution of the senses can also make the imaginary world real based on certain experiences that do not come under the purview of senses! *There is nobody to trick a mind it tricks by itself.*

318. A *concept* has significance only to those who created or understood it. Similarly a *belief* can have meaning only to those who believed or experienced it.

319. *Stupidity* is a natural way of tackling *nature* and often it turns out to be a better if not the best option!

320. *Nature* fools a *man* first and achieves its purpose, by the time he gains intelligence and looks back on how he was deceived it is no longer the same nature! It is a different nature now; for him the game starts afresh again.

321. *Good and intelligence*: being *good* is enormously difficult compared to being *intelligent*. The measure of intelligence is shallow, broad and originates at *brain* and that of good is deep and subtle and has its sources at *heart*. Therefore it is possible for more men to be intelligent than good!

322. The inherent nature of *materialistic progress* is that it makes man's mind aware of one thing and ignorant of ten other things; materials restrict the reach of the mind and hence the positive ways of working.

323. More than anything else, the existence of these *two* often leads to contradictions: *man and God!*

324. A man would like *God* much more if he knows very well that God did not exist. If the existence of God is confirmed man's first job would be to make sure that '*He*' became extinct and only then would man start to love him. *It easier and safer for the human mind to start to love with non-existing things. Man somehow becomes an enemy of existing things and a friend of extinct entities!*

325. The most *powerful* and least powerful man would do the same kind of mischief. The former thinks he has nothing further to gain and the latter thinks he has nothing further to lose. However if they think in exactly the opposite way, it would be good for the both of them.

326. If a man thinks of 'something' or someone as *divine* and *sacred*, he is already fooled. This can happen to anybody as long as he is not fully aware of that something! There always exits a gap in awareness or 'distance' that does the trick. *Distance makes an idiot appear as intelligent and the same way an ordinary and profane one as sacred!*

327. *Good* and *bad* are the most useful of all human misunderstandings. Both actually originate from the understanding of something and misunderstanding of the same thing!

328. *Intelligent* man creates *God* and destroys the same thousands of times during his lifetime. Obviously, *idiots* also do the same, but a fewer number of times.

329. *Man* is nature's greatest discovery and *God* is man's cheapest invention.

330. In primitive societies when the human *mind* was simple, *nature* was complex enough to threaten him. Now, once he has come to understand nature and deal with the follies of nature, his own mind has become complex and threatens him.

331. A man should befriend his own mind before he actually develops a *friendship* with another man.

332. Yesterday's *knowledge* has already become stupid, today's knowledge will become so by tomorrow and it can never become knowledge again. Hence *a transition from one level of stupidity to another level is being claimed as progress in knowledge.*

333. Until one man meets another there are no *politics*.

334. When socialization starts very early on in childhood, it is the instinct of *power* that manifests first, much before reason!

335. The words '*power*' and '*shame*' are close friends and can be found more frequently in *politics* than in any other fields of human venture.

336. *Idiots* either overdo or under do; the idea of balancing is not known to them, because they were idiots already.

337. The language of *nature* is electromagnetic waves; if there exists anything subtler than these, they would be another type of wave similar to electromagnetic waves but with different frequency and wavelength. As such *words* and *worlds* are made up of differing frequencies and wavelengths.

338. It is natural that all men and women try to acquire material since they need it. In case of *idiots*, the mind is full of material while for the *intelligent* the mind makes material. This is because an intelligent man knows the quantum of requirement better than any idiot and his relation with it. As such the relationship between the human mind and materials become one of the most dominant factors that decide the very fabric of human nature apart from historically well-established social relations. *The intelligent men handle the materials while the same materials handle idiots.*

339. *Society* is a huge opportunity for brave and genuine individuals and a big distress for weak men.

340. The *real* world always tends to become unreal once the human mind tries to define it, by the time it finishes the definition the *real* becomes a fully *unreal*. This way the

'real' is left alone without any definition. However, in the process it turned out to be a *feeling* of the defining mind, often the best feelings!

341. How to *keep quiet* is definitely difficult but when to keep quiet is even more difficult.

342. *The mind* cheats man unless he has a reason strong enough to force it to commit. It is better to dictate his own mind as often as possible, instead of wasting time on other activities; mind plays the role of servant better. In actual practice any human mind first longs for a master, if no one is found it becomes a master and misbehaves, if the *reason* is inadequate. Again if the reason is abundant then the very reason starts misbehaving or misleading the mind!

343. *Thinking* about the *future* is not only a good dream but is a great strategy of the mind to escape from present misery.

344. *Perfection* cannot exist; existence inherently involves imperfection. Perfection can only be a subjective dream. However, in the name of perfection it is not uncommon for some minds to fool themselves in a pleasurable way.

345. A *capitalistic* society makes *women 'commodities'*. The women who cannot escape from this fact alone try to increase their sales value: it is this value that renders either comfort or consolation.

346. Power is basic to human nature; even this basic human instinct of *power* is only with respect to other men, i.e., *outside* of him. However, *knowledge* has to be necessarily *within* him. *Therefore any real protection for a man has to come only from within.* If a man meets another more

powerful man he cannot increase his original power. But if he meets a man of more knowledge his knowledge also increases! *Thus knowledge is a power by itself. Knowledge is the mind's way of convincing itself not with respect to other minds.* But absolute knowledge is doubtful: it is certainly unfair and unreasonable for a man to claim absolute knowledge with the help of the five human senses working under one unsteady master.

347. *God* is a *revelation* for few and *ignorance* for many.

348. As soon as a man becomes conscious of his *stupidity* he exerts himself to attach and accumulate money, power and popularity as compensation.

349. *Intentions* are infinitely more powerful than rituals. Ultimately, it is the intention that shows the destination, later understood as the *destiny*.

350. One's *ignorance* is all others' business.

351. A man who *hides* more than what he reveals would fall faster than what he intends to hold onto.

352. Finally, *knowledge* only wins. Further, in the world of practice *prudence* shows that *belief* also as a kind of knowledge!

353. The *reality* for *average men* is what he has been made to like, he is not bothered about whether it exists inside of him or what exists out there.

354. The human *mind* makes concepts or '*ideas*' that guide us to understand the world. Interestingly the same ideas have their origin only in our earlier misunderstandings. *Nature* tricks a man's mind all the time; every time any

understanding happens, he already seems to have been sitting on a misunderstanding!

355. *Reason* is not fully independent of instinct at any point in time. This is due to the fact that reason is also a kind of *instinct* only. *Reason is an instinct aware of its own actions!* Again the *awareness* is not helpful and advantageous to a large section of human beings; reason is not able to defend and protect the masses from the dreadfulness of nature. The awareness imparted by reason rarely leads to knowledge; instead more often it leads to a fearful existence. The worst is, men want to get rid of awareness itself and abandon reason forcing the mind to drift and wander in search of imaginary things that do not warrant application of reason.

    Such imaginary world gives an easy escape route and becomes more blissful than the real world; the destitute mind is smart enough to create a blissful entity, the God, to administer its own imaginary world. Despite the existence of God frustrations occur in the imaginary world and the mind quickly reconciles since all the settings of the imaginary world are its own creation. The mind cannot implicate anybody in the imaginary world as it does in the real world. God is very much there, but the mind cannot blame its own creation!

356. *Love* is the most *real* amongst all unreal!

357. Men may not be conscious about their own *prejudice;* however, each man is unique and distinguished only by his prejudice.

358. Finally what any *rationalist* should understand is that the *'irrational'* that holds the sway; mighty nature is

forever waiting to trap or allure a man and one fine day it certainly traps!

359. A *man* with intense *love* will be either in hell or heaven for sure, nothing in between. But if he did not love anything until now he is yet to understand his own nature, yet to start his life!

360. Powerful *women* are less *democratic* than *men*. The power affects, relatively, women's minds more permanently than men's minds. I leave this fact to the readers to confirm *empirically*.

361. One can say that not taking a *decision* is also a decision; but most of the times it turns out to be a wrong decision! Indecision is indecision first, it is only a stupid man's trick that later acquires the status of a decision. Indecision is a weak man's *trick* designed and kept waiting for chance, if any, for its success.

362. *God* is a beautiful idea. When one is in distress and despair the same idea seems more beautiful, admirable and beneficial than all other kinds of ideas and imaginations. Distress being a mental state, it becomes essential for the mind to create another mental state to overcome it, hence god.

363. Human beings are the same for all practical purposes, but for *culture* and its influence; the *belief* systems of all societies are essentially a manifestation of deeply underlying *instincts* whose owner is *nature*.

364. *Keeping quiet* amounts to a thousand rituals; it only demands a bit of intelligence but quite a lot of patience.

365. *Woman* is mind, *man* is body; naturally they cannot be expected to exist independent of each other. Interestingly,

a stupid person understands this fact fast while the intelligent argues this wastefully.

366. *Nature* alone has the power to justify wrong as a right!

367. The rate at which *money* affects a man is inversely proportional to his *intelligence*.

368. The rate at which *power* affects a man is directly proportional to his *stupidity*.

369. A bit on *power* and *money*: both may look like close allies and hence a man may mistake this as being interchangeable; but it is actually not so. Power is one of the most original of all human instincts and money is one of its components, it need not always be a necessary component. The power is a master and money is only a slave. If a powerful man accumulates money, he simply aims for more slaves. If money buys power, then the master is too weak!

370. Human behaviour is not mathematically amenable; yet this equation can be applied: *Instinct* + *culture* = *morality*.

371. When there is no *memory*, there is no human mind.

372. A man is definitely *intelligent* until such time he happens to understand his *own stupidity*; but in many cases that never happens! This is because either the world around him behaves to make him or he himself behaves to suit the world to validate that he is intelligent.

373. A man who marries a woman, begets children and undergoes *normal life* patiently with the cycle of happiness-sorrow is infinitely superior to the saints and seers who claim, again only claim, dubiously, their

closeness to God. *Normal life abundantly demonstrates the least distraction of the human mind, its closeness to nature and often nature itself!*

374. Both *Politics* and *Spiritualism* are formal and informal ways of one man's attempt to rule over the minds of other men. I feel the former is better than the latter in the sense of transparency and accountability.

375. *Spiritualism* is a direct feeling and the subsequent awareness that happens is immensely beneficial *only* for individuals. Accordingly, any collective practice of spiritualism is inherently exploitative since another man comes in to paint the picture. In the real world the strong minds incline towards the former and the weaker minds opt for the latter.

376. *Culture* regulates human instincts in physical terms in the form of art, films, festivals etc. Similarly, *spiritualism* also can regulate human instincts in so many mental terms. But both do the business of the regulation and guidance only to the extent that profoundly strong human nature itself would admit and there ends the role of both culture and spiritualism; any attempt to kill the *original instinct* would only make men more dubious. As such those attempts will only be a *claim* not an achievement. *History can have records in abundance of some men fooling some others, but never a single man did so the same with nature.*

377. *Trust* is the starting point of exploitation. Any religion first forces a man to trust! In *politics the* weak exploit the weaker; in *business* stupid exploits stupider people; it all becomes feasible only due to *trust*, existing already or created for a specific purpose.

378. Men made *society* first for the sake of security. Subsequently defined the *good* and the *bad* in the name of morality. Finally cunningness and reason led to exploitation. Otherwise, the inherently exploitive nature all our *social institutions* cannot be accounted for!

379. It is not prudent to believe in the man who preaches against *nature*. Nature is the master preacher and those who go against it are finally found to be cheats.

380. The mind of a woman is more natural than the one of the man and that makes, in general, *women* less dubious than *men*. Yet blind nature knows how to balance this imbalance; it makes a particular woman far more dubious than hundreds of men!

381. It is man who made the *good* and the *bad* without consulting *nature*. For this mistake he pays a royalty throughout his life.

382. Any *religion* in its pure form is the best source of knowledge and closer to the mind and experience. However, the practical formats of religions are nothing more than a bundle of convenient and comfortable lies.

383. Individually, *spiritualism* is a fantastic feeling capable of healing one's mind. But collectively, it would make men sick, religion becomes really deceptive and often it goes against a person's own progressive nature.

384. *Idiots* often turn out to be very skilful.

385. On an average, ordinary men have greater *virtues* than the so called extraordinary men. But there is nothing here to be proud of since the former is a necessity and the latter is encouraged by acquired circumstances.

386. A *man* who stands by the side of *nature* has few worries.

387. Both *reason* and *intuition* can never contradict each other in their usefulness, except for idiots and eccentric men. Reason and intuition are really meant to perform complementary and supplementary roles.

388. *Freedom*: for an individual, the real benefit of freedom comes from subsequent *restraint*; otherwise the freedom becomes the most futile of all other futile possessions.

389. A man's permanent *enemy* always appreciates him; who don't do so is an enemy, but not permanent! What about *friends*? The first category is apparently felt and claimed as being friends! Again it is only a claim, pending for validation. Such claims may often have their origins in the form of societal requirements or some sort of compulsion. Hence, *friendship* is largely sponsored by society but *enmity* is a natural tendency born along with instinct!

390. Often the *truth* turns out to be a theoretical aspect of various practical aspects called *lies*.

391. If this universe consists of multiple things, then tracing the origin of such multiplicity necessarily leads to *nothing*. If the nothing is found to be the source of origin then *nothing* is the answer for everything! The world can only permit *many things* or *nothing*.

392. It is no wonder that everyone *acts or pretends*, but no one does it as perfectly as the *modern sages do*. By modern sages I mean those who either preach for amazing wealth or protecting the existing wealth; they understood fellow men better than the *nature* that they supposed to understand! Above all they have *enough time and little responsibility* to make their actions better than the

rest. These modern sages only invented a spiritualism according which accumulating wealth is bliss!

393. Ultimately, it is *intention* that finishes a man off; one cannot escape from his own intentions.

394. *Mysteries* are an idiot's ways of looking at nature; mystery is nature's way of bogging down any man. Again, *intelligence* is only a *relative* term, with respect to another man. Hence, for this reason an intelligent man, however great he may be, also encounters mysteries, but in less numbers.

395. A *woman's mind* is most subtle in the world; its opposite also should be true!

396. In general, an *advice* between *men* to men is less sincere than the one between women to *women*. But the most sincere, genuine and reliable are the ones either from men to women and vice versa.

397. In general, *angry women* are more virtuous than the rest!

398. In life, when one encounters a thousand women of easy virtue, there occurs a single *woman* whose *conviction* and principles keep alive the expectations and imaginations of two thousand men. In this way, throughout the history of existence, a few women are able to *impact* a disproportionately large number of men.

399. *Democracy* is simply a series of dramas. The special feature of it is that everyone has an *opportunity* to act in some role or the other till he becomes tired. When he becomes tired he is satisfied. The existence of 'that opportunity' keeps democracy going.

400. *Art* and *immorality* are close cousins.

401. *Immorality* knocks on the door if someone who has power, money and popularity far in excess of his capacity to manage it. But there are exceptions, those who are not willing to open the door.

402. Immediate *popularity* makes a man believe that he is more intelligent than the rest. Popularity slowly makes an enduring friendship only with the stupidity around. In general, popularity restricts vision, kills common sense and breeds ill.

403. *Spiritualism* is very much possible without God. In fact this will slowly become a reality in the future. As society becomes more and more civilized and women become more and more rational, spiritualism without God will become more reasonable and acceptable to the mind. *All are in mind.*

404. An *ordinary man* with a few masks is superior to a *holy* man with a thousand masks.

405. The original and natural instinct behind the origin of *culture* should have been 'an intention to possess' particularly in the male species. Hence among human beings, men are only responsible for creation and also the sustenance of culture in the present form.

406. *Idiots* do unsustainable things. The reverse is equally true; one becomes an idiot by doing unsustainable things.

407. In real life, advisers need more *advice* than the advised; unfortunately the same is not available to them at right time!

408. In any society it is the *man-woman relationship* that is primary and decides all other innumerable relations.

409. In theory, *religion* should be more useful than *science*. But in practice religion is more quickly understood or misunderstood yet always misused compared to the sciences; only few people can misuse the latter. Hence the world of human history shows us the loss and exploitation of humanity due to religion was always found to be more than the loss and misuse of science if reported correctly!

410. A man's *worst enemy* is a thousand times better than a modern '*god-man*' whose life is clouded in secrecy; yet that man believes himself as divine. Nature's job is to make us differently, as such there nothing more to invent. *There is no 'holiness' without transparency.*

411. All conscious men can be thought of as spiritual beings. The essence of spiritualism is a belief system, irrespective of whether they believe in god or not. One set of belief systems can force a man to believe in god and another set of belief systems makes yet another man disbelieve god. Ultimately both can be claimed as correct. *Each man's game has his own rules; the result of a game resides within its rules.*

412. Often '*scarcity*' becomes the starting point of *idealism* and '*inability*' the starting point of *perversion*.

413. *Astrology* is a subject where the answers are right even though the equations are wrong! *It is a game played after fully knowing the result.*

414. *Science* is more close to nature without knowing what nature is and *religion* is more close to God without knowing who God is. The beauty of science lies in its efforts to *explain* the imperfect and the usefulness of religion lies in *claiming* perfection in imperfection.

415. The *good* and *bad* are dependent on two factors: one, primarily it is quantitative; second, secondarily it depends on a particular perspective.

416. The world is not a big deal for any individual but for dealing with his own *conscience. One cannot sell conscience on one side and project strength and honour on the other side.* After all, whatever *good* a man does with all his personal 'advertising' should have been done quietly by someone already. In the same way whatever *bad* being done now 'secretly' also would have been blatantly done by some man long before!

417. There is no worth in blaming any *belief system* after all a belief is as real as the stupidity that gave birth to it. Every belief system is a world in itself.

418. A man thinks himself as a beggar or a king; another man is actually a beggar or a king, then there is no difference between both of them; *mind* only matters.

419. From human perspective all natural creations are based on *inequalities*, between the species and also within the species. Those who aware of this would say that nature is blind and chaotic. But some others may say that nature has a *purpose* and the inequality itself is carefully *designed*. Both groups are aware of nature in their own way; it is their way of looking at the same thing, as such nobody can be blamed.

From the above, one thing becomes clear. If something is true for someone, its opposite also has to be true for some other at least. *This is because we always define 'something' in such a way that its opposite also comes into existence.* Again we have no other ways of defining anything and forcing to conclude that *if something is true its opposite also has to be true.* For example say, if science teaches that all matters emit electromagnetic radiation, we can very well create another stand in which all matter is created only by electromagnetic radiation and still call it science. Both work!

What I mean is that all the physical processes are actually two-way processes. But we often have the capacity to look at one way or one perspective and be indifferent to if not opposed to the other equally valid perspective.

420. *Chicken-egg problem* is not that complicated to solve! The chicken and the egg always existed simultaneously. Whatever existed before the chicken was not an egg of the chicken and whatever existed before the egg was not actually a chick of the egg! Nature has no time and hence things occur simultaneously, but for the routine human perspective. As such the chicken-egg conundrum happens only due to a particular human perspective, which makes one thing as preceding and other as succeeding.

421. *Ego* is not necessary because no one understands it; again ego becomes a necessity for the same reason!

422. In *life*, a man is satisfying his ego, often unconsciously and inevitably.

423. *Matter* should necessarily come out of nothing, visually nothing! Alternatively it can be said that at all other times it should vanish into nothing. Hence for all practical purposes nothing creates everything.

424. Excepting for the *stories* created in and around him by himself, a man is really insignificantly and inconsequently

small in this universe. But the stories work as long as the force behind the stories is not known.

425. Thoughts and intentions have to travel; if not the theory of *karma* cannot work and therefore religions are not feasible.

426. *Men* or *women* either do or intention to do the same mischief, peculiar to their physical and mental make-up; what is understood as *attitude* is how differently they do the same thing.

427. Popularity is the servant of *money*. Money is the servant of *power*. If all men are classified into two orders of idiots, the first orders of idiots are slaves of popularity and the second order are slaves of money. If a third order is possible, the intelligent ones among idiots, they would come under slaves of power.

428. Depending on a man's mental makeup, '*science*' and '*religion*' are nothing more two different ways of looking at *nature* while actually there exists infinite ways of looking at the same nature. Nature depends on the nature of human contemplation itself.

429. A man's *fate* or destiny is decided by decisions that he takes 'for' and 'against' his *conscience*. After the appearance of *reason* among human beings and its subsequent assemblage of conscience, the man of reason perpetually battles with his own conscience compared to any other conceivable entity either in hell or in heaven.

Honestly, a man of reason respects no one except his conscience; only in that process of respecting his own conscience all the others in and around him receive the respect *due* to them. *Conscience is more benevolent than God and much more dangerous than any demon!*

430. In general, the *power* affects a *man* in more or less consistent and predictable ways but a *woman* in more erratic ways.

431. *Beauty* is not in the eye but in the mind of beholder. Here, the involvement of the mind makes man take a bit extra *time* to understand this fact. Only a hurried mind fixes the blame on the senses.

432. If all the people are made to tell same and similar lies at the same time it is *religion*. If one man tells a unique lie at one point in time it is *science*, of course with a lot of hard work to substantiate it.

433. A man is in trouble or disorder due his own 'internal contradictions'. The *contradictions* arise at least from two major sources. One is *'biologically given'* and the other is a *'sociological necessity'*. The latter is the same for all members of society and hence all have more or less some pain or pleasure; but each man devices his own escape route. But the former, the biologically given is largely attributed and interpreted as *fate*.

434. All human creations are in fact their own reactions to the actions and influences on their *minds*. Who acts on their own mind is the *world*, near and far both known and unknown.

435. *Business* is a cyclic process that starts with a *lie* and ends with the *truth*.

436. *Art is an illusion within an illusion.* As a man grows up in the initial stages he slowly understands everything

around him as an illusion; as time passes his mind is doubtful of its earlier understanding and therefore decides to get out of such temporary and transient surroundings. This inevitably leads to a more permanent '*mental arrangements*' in order to calm his mind; idealism is born this way. Again, the mind behaves this way duly forgetting the fact that the very mental circumstances have origin in the same illusive physical surroundings. Even after creating its own 'mental world' the mind never takes rest but tries to validate it; with an intention to validate the human mind looks out in the world of illusion where it started initially to match its mental world only to find that the mental world is more elusive than the real world. Art is such a *mental construction*, an illusion within an illusion. It is true that initially the effect of art is soothing and pleasurable but *finally*, one can certainly anticipate art to disturb and distress and leave a human mind defenceless in real world.

437. *Reason's* single most important responsibility is to control, regulate and tame the power, the natural instinct; without the aid of reason, a powerful man is blind to his responsibility. Reason is the guiding force and the *torch bearer* of the otherwise blind power.

438. *Freedom* is a mind's ultimate purpose, but not for all, the unwarranted freedom available to *masses* and few others *elite* who lack reason can only lead to destruction. The masses in general have inadequate reason while few elite have weak reasoning powers in comparison to their status and wealth. In all, such situations freedom is not at their service and hence useless. Instead it positively destructs their peaceful existence by creating a mental imbalance,

often not fully known to them. In case of the elite such freedom is a silent killer particularly when it conjoins with perversion, as both instantly become intimate friends. Interestingly this happens more in *democracy,* the birthplace of unguided freedom. *Freedom kills more people than war.*

439. *Power* is superior to *money;* the former enables one man to control others directly while the latter intends to do the same in an indirect way, often less successfully.

440. *Power* and *popularity* tend to make a man deviant. Again, powerful men are less deviant than the popular ones! This is because the power has much more responsibility than what popularity does. But what about a man without any power, as he would hardly have any responsibility, he would all the time *tend* to do the same mischief as the popular ones whether he actually does it or not.

441. *Government*: in a democratic form of government the number of Acts and the quantum rules required for governance of a state represents the nature of the citizens, how they are 'deviant socially' and 'stupid naturally'! The existence of more rules not only show how stupid the *ruled but also the rulers.*

442. *Fear*: when fear grips an intelligent man he argues, defends, justifies, etc. his actions and wastes time. But if fear seizes an idiot he straight away goes to worship god.

443. *Hell and heaven*: the stupidity of a man first creates *good* and *bad. This distinction is local, i.e.* at the terrestrial level, with a limited utility. When the stupidity brims over, it does so in the form of *hell* and *heaven* as its celestial counterparts. The hell and heaven are in fact created

simultaneously in a person's mind and as such there came in to existence a *connection* between them during the creation itself and hence both are always connected since the time of inception.

This way a human mind not only creates *hell* and *heaven* but due its wandering nature it has to necessarily travel between them along the already available connecting route! Two human minds actually differ. The only difference between any two human minds is how frequently they travel between hell and heaven. The frequency of travel and duration of stay in any one place is largely controlled by an individual's very inner nature and his mind's reaction to external influences.

The external influence, all the things that exist outside of human mind, manipulates one's own inner nature. While the manipulation of his inner nature sometimes happen wilfully and consciously by himself, quite often it happens without his full awareness and hence things become beyond his control. Stupidity wants heaven for its own sake. But while creating *heaven a man's stupidity is unaware of a simultaneous creation of hell; even if it is aware of hell it does not foresee the birth of the connecting path that the human mind has to necessarily use!* Therefore finally a human mind cannot avoid travelling between hell and heaven, its own creation.

When a human mind creates something, its opposite is also being created at some other corner of his mind. If he creates heaven, he also creates hell yet he may become conscious of hell only later.

444. No *social service* is ever done by collecting people, but rather done for the usage of others for self-satisfaction if

not building self-image. True service arises in man only out of his own, standalone, understanding of himself.

445. If at all anything has to be *real*, then it has to be within a man's mind; the real is as subjective as his consciousness. *External nature* that one looks at depends on his nature; again it finally turns out to be his understanding of his own nature.

446. *Love*: it is naturally 'possible' for one man to love one or more women; evidently the same is true for a woman. These obvious facts never help to understand the very nature of love. Despite the obvious, there will be a juncture in which it is 'not at all possible' for one 'not to love' the other even after repeated positive attempts; only at this juncture a man is taught the real nature of love. As such *the true nature of love is understood by a man or woman not from numerous possible actions but from one impossible act!*

447. Reason is the architect of human *conscience*. Once the building is built the architect disappears into the same building! Of the three components that constitute conscience, the *instinct*, *reason* and *culture*, it is reason that plays a conscious role in constructing a fairly acceptable and enduring conscience. Within conscience instinct is dominant, reason is important and culture plays only supportive role. Reason after fully developing the conscience seamlessly blends with it.

448. *Man* is intelligent enough to create a *god* at some time and stupid enough to search for the god at some other time!

449. *Ultimately those who do not believe in god are as stupid as those who believe in it*. Knowingly or unknowingly, both

categories of men perpetually clinging to an eccentric, yet more comfortable and convincing view than other similar possible views. The 'comfortable and convincing view' arises due to the respective mind's 'specific' capability to understand nature and its surroundings. *God is the handiwork work of the mind.*

Therefore, at least a little knowledge of how a man's mind works is necessary before understanding the issue of *god*. Either logically or illogically a mind continuously works only to suit its own comfort as its end product. The *basic nature of mind attached to human beings is that it has no 'rigid' stand in any of the world issues but for its comfort and convenience*. Strangely, the little stupid mind attached to man not only has a capability to support and justify its earlier stands but also to destroy some or all of its earlier views! This way a *prejudiced mind makes a slave to itself.* But the prejudice itself, which forbids the mind from freedom, was created by the mind in its earlier circumstances that warranted a comfort and convenience.

The ever changing mind actually keeps creating and destroying many things all the time. Hence, according to any *individual* man's true nature of mind, *God exists sometimes and does not exist at some other times. A man clinging to only one stand definitely feels 'convenient and comfortable' most of the times but it is also true that he 'tortures himself' the rest of the time.*

450. The followers of *religion* always outnumber those who do not. This is because *reason* demands proof and logic but *belief* requires only a convenient, mental state. A belief is an *acceptance* and hence it is an easy mental process, pending his own ability for proof or until he is convinced

about someone else's proof about the existence of god. But disbelief involves a positive act of *rejection* with the help of reason involving hard mental labour.

451. The question '*why*' of a man's actions leads to endless questions and finally to *despair* without any satisfactory answer.

452. *Intelligence* is bliss but is scarce, uncertain and unavailable to the masses. However *nature* works differently: it makes ignorance bliss. Nature does the same through many routes: one of most popular routes is, *love*; here nature makes a man or *woman* as stupid, as often as possible, to dictate its own idea. During the initial stages, *nature* dominates man's reason and logic and makes them incapable of questioning the actions of brute force the nature and hence the love not only arises but also sustains. But, subsequently when the concerned man becomes aware of his stupidity, if not his ignorance, the woman had already understood, accepted his stupidity without bothering about her own!

453. *Instinct* is a master and a blind monster. I do not intend to call it a stupid master because it is our primary nature. The master has two servants: one is, '*reason*' a dwarf servant but definitely an intelligent one. Here, whether the reason is good or bad is not relevant, after all being a servant it frequently accedes to the master's ways, if not all the time. The '*belief*', is another servant of the master who is for ever committed to being more stupid than the other servant, reason. After all any master likes the stupid servant more often than the intelligent one, the reason, whose views are heard occasionally.

454. It is obvious that during earlier periods, say before the advent of science and its subsequent progress, *women* tried to possess assets and wealth not only for usage but also for security. Further women also wanted *men* to manage the difficult affairs of the capital thereby restricting their own role to the easy usage! This, over the years led men to have a strong intention and attitude associating the possession of capital with women. Accordingly I firmly believe, from the point of view of men, possession of *women* would have preceded all other possessions. Hence, the starting point of *capitalism* that advocates private property as its central theme can be found by tracing back this fact, the possession of women by men. This way a woman became the starting point of capitalism!

455. *Human society* works through the simple fact that in each and every issue there always exists a *disagreement or contrary view* among the members of the society, however small it may be, whether the persons concerned are aware, recognize it or not.

456. In *general*, a *woman* feels more of mind and a *man* tries to be more consciousness of things around. This fact frequently makes the man project his intelligence and the woman shows her emotion.

457. *Death* causes only the subjective *consciousness* to vanish; since a man is not the owner of his *mind* it does not get affected! The consciousness is an individualistic view of mind while the master mind itself is wide spread and exists everywhere.

458. *Intelligence* is due to a man's brain process capable of understanding the small mind attached to human beings;

but *intuition* is a feeling received by the small mind when it aligns itself with the larger mind that goes far beyond human physical existence.

459. *Man* and woman: if both are *rational* their relationship will be unstable and often destructive. If both are *irrational* they will be defenceless making themselves vulnerable and accessible to exploitation by others. Generally, *a rational man and irrational woman make the best possible relationship*; the other way around can't be the best because originally men created culture by thinking that women will be forever irrational. Interestingly most men still believe this to be so!

460. *Freedom and morality*: the origin of morality can be traced to either biological or sociological or both, ultimately it is freedom that gives birth to morality. Even if the morality is biologically anterior to freedom the latter has power to modify the former. As such the first son of freedom is *morality* while its second son is *immorality!* Freedom ensures a man can have discretion to behave any possible way he chooses to do so. A man desires freedom for these purposes only. Except for this *covert purpose*, human freedom has no other practical utility.

461. *Power* may have abundant opportunities to laugh at everything; but finally and decisively it is *knowledge* that laughs at power!

462. *Men* are same; *women* are differently same!

463. All man-made political systems tend to treat *women* as commodities, but it is only in capitalism that women treat themselves as commodities. Further it is *capitalism* that ensures more resale value to women! Often it becomes,

directly or indirectly, the job of men is to fix the values for the sellers and buyers. *Capitalism sells everything including human nature!*

464. *Man* is the greatest disorder within nature, without a man *nature* would be less chaotic.

465. *Idiots* quickly discover *order* in *disorder* but an intelligent person detects, with added risk and labour, disorder in order often only to trouble himself.

466. *Virtue* is in the genes of all women and occurs by chance for men, if at all.

467. Even if god exists, it can never be perceived as intelligent; the human mind does not *intend* a god to be intelligent, but rather for god to be good and pleasing.

468. *Capitalism* is nothing but the unfolding of all basic human instincts; *Democracy* provides a basic theoretical justification necessary for it. *Democracy is a pre-supposed theory*, with a cunning theme called *freedom*, to accommodate *capitalism*, the originally intended purpose.

469. It is *morality* versus *power:* if the *powerful* and *powerless* are like two adjacent mountains, then morality is a thin steam flowing in a valley in between. The thin stream repeatedly depletes and dries out, but the water course remains because both the mountains remain!

470. If *Art* is considered as whole of the moon, then only what appears as the thin yet bright crescent is *morality*.

471. *Art* is a gateway to immorality; certainly the gate is beautifully designed.

472. *Art*, *religion*, *science* are different tools accessible to individual minds to deal more with themselves than the world outside.

473. By the time a man realises that his mind is not fitting with the people around him, he has already become a *leader*. As such *a leader is never a part of the crowd called followers*.

474. This is one way of connecting *science* and *religion* that otherwise antagonises to each other: *culture* is the daughter of *religion* and *civilization* is the son of *science*. One is conservative hence not ready to change while the other is liberal always anticipating a change; yet both of them meet as lovers do while their parents never meet!

475. *Art* and *science: Art* effortlessly lifts a man's mind off the ground and dumps it often in a far-flung location and that too in an unexpected way. Art is a delightful and seductive teacher, but it never teaches the real world and thus makes minds vulnerable. However, *Science* talks tough and takes the mind step by step, of course with the associated little pains; in the process it makes the mind experience and encounter the real world of phenomena without much distress. Science is a hard teacher, but its lesson is realistic.

476. In genuine and sustainable human relations *forgetting* is as important as *remembering* if not more.

477. *Disorder* has many authors: the abundance of freedom, money and power; also in that order.

478. *Accident* is an event and *design* is process that happens in between the events.

479. After *love* a man is never the same, love makes stupid men intelligent and intelligent one as stupid!

480. When a man is in *love*, her absence makes him as a poet; her presence makes him a scientist.

481. Mostly for men, *love* begins from a glimpse of the face and ends with the mind!

482. A man who is single has no *culture*.

483. *God* exists but never advertises; man would be extinct without advertising.

484. Theoretically and also actually, *democracy* allows more criminals than any other political system; further the multitude like this fact due to the very same reason.

485. The visible, invisible, already understood and yet to be understood altogether constitute a *reality*. Thus always there is an element of uncertainty in reality.

486. *Originally*, again originally, the scientific lies were *terrestrial* while the religious lies were *celestial* and thus making the latter more attractive than the former.

487. *Democracy*, in general, is against nature; women are more natural than men. Despite these facts, strangely, democracy affects men more than women! There a reason to believe that men by heart do not want to be democratic!!

488. Most powerful *women* are madly undemocratic; the most probable reason is the impatient mind. Why the impatience when women are mostly noted for their patience? The *power* necessarily brings in numerous matters and disputes simultaneously. Most women are

naturally excellent in handling at few issues at a time, but not at confronting many dilemmas and conflicts. Under normal circumstances, women are at their best in controlling their minds much better than men do, when too many issues crop up at a time, the best possible strategy is, be undemocratic! This is an empirical fact.

489. A *beauty* is as vulnerable as it is valuable.

490. All *visible* things have its own invisible supportive structure. For instance, every *intention* is built on its equal and opposite intention buried underneath either by nature or by reason. In the same way *good* is necessarily built on or founded on *bad* whether the builder is aware of this or not. Behind any good always precedes an awareness and understanding of bad; as such the bad becomes a supportive structure of the good! A man is supported by woman; a man cannot be defined in isolation without any reference to a woman. Yet this dichotomy is valid only in the 'sense based' physical and practical world; this discontinuity is a projection of nature by senses for a functional purpose, while the continuous nature at large is hidden behind!

491. Originally, *men* wanted to possess while *women* wanted to be protected. Men's desire for possession made him active and risky but women's desire for security was passive; this way the proactive nature of men's ambition automatically took care of the passive needs of women. Obviously that led men to more distress than women. Today things have changed a lot. But the basic problem remains the same for both men and women: a*n intention to possess leads to distress and despair.*

492. *Democracy* often gives freedom to people only to make them undemocratic.

493. The ill of *democracy* is that it relies more on proof than facts; in other words it brings into existence material which is perceived as being more important and influential than the *mind*.

494. The real *progress* of a society depends on how many men really understand a woman's mind!

495. *Spiritualism* is definitely not a license to lie; it is neither a business proposition nor the gateway to madness!

496. Mind and nature*: mind is the nature and nature is the mind*. The same one has been given two names. The world perceptible to human senses is understood as nature while the one that directs the senses is mind. This is because the human senses are positioned in between mind and nature. The very position and functioning of senses apparently makes nature and mind as two distinct entities.

497. *Love* is the first *revolution* that happens in the 'human' mind*; it is authored by nature, instigated by instinct and implemented by desire*. Love makes a human mind subdued of reason and hence incapable of controlling the two agents of mighty nature: *instinct* and the *desire*. By the time reason understands the real reason behind the revolution, it becomes irreversible and reason is forced to justify if not support love!

498. It is true that *reason* teaches the width and depth of the physical world but it is *love* that shows how deep the human mind itself is.

499. The importance of *thinking* lies in the very thinking itself.

500. *Life* is unfolding of the *mind* through the *brain*; hence it is as subjective as the physiology of the individual brain!

501. *Men* misuse *freedom*; for *women* it is the other way around.

502. Intending to do something and speaking some other thing is the heart and soul of *politics*!

503. History shows *religious* exploitation as being deep-rooted and severe compared to *social* and *economic* exploitation. The basic and yet the strange reason is: everywhere the intelligent can exploit idiots but it is only in religion that idiots can very well exploit idiots! In the *social* sphere also one can think of idiots exploiting idiots however they would hide behind *status*; in the economic and political spheres they would do so with *wealth* and *power* respectively.

504. *Men* are very good at *reason;* but *women* are more *reasonable* than men!

505. If the first glance is ugly and unpleasant then the repeated looks at the same thing or the same one make it better and acceptable, if the first look is beautiful and appealing then the repeated looks make it less and less beautiful. A man hardly has any control over this fact because repeated perception *always* makes a man's understanding and aesthetics move from *culture* to *nature*.

506. *Religious lies* are numerically dominant in comparison to all other forms of lies yet its *usefulness* provide a firm foundation for its maintenance and sustainability of such a huge pile of lies for such long human history. The *lies*

in the name *religion* are of immediate relief to the mind and are always a huge hit among idiots! But such lies were originally created mostly by a little group of idiots who pretended to be intelligent. It is true that they were intelligent enough to create such *usefulness* in the lies! In case of *culture*, the *lies* are created by irrational yet intelligent men similar to the same target idiots as said in religion above.

507. One cannot be *reasonable* twice for the same issue!

508. A man is *reasonable* only to the extent that he is *comfortable*; hence being reasonable tacitly points to an intention, to be both comfortable and agreeable!

509. It is known that an *idle mind* is the most creative. Accordingly a jobless fellow can have more radical ideas than those at work! But to implement and make the ideas acceptable to others he has to do a lot more work!

510. *Love* does no injustice; because love by itself is *justice*.

511. *Justice* is external and *love* internal; thus *love* is more fundamental and the primary aspect of justice. Hence without some kind of a love no justice is possible. In case of *society*, love only manifests as *reason* to do its best in the form of justice!

512. *Virtue* and *morality* are complex functions of biology, individual freedom and social circumstances.

513. *Nature* is irrational.

514. *Religion* is a theory and *culture* is a practical extension of it.

515. *Irrationality* is like an ocean and rationality, that is *reason*, is like the *currents* in the ocean. The 'ocean currents' are

regular and periodical. Even though the currents occur due external influences like season and temperature etc. they remain a part of the ocean only; the influence of ocean streams on climate is well known. Similarly, the *reason* that manifests according to external causes like logic and science remains connected to the irrational *mind* only. Like the ocean currents the reason is also regular and periodical. In brief, reason is only a tiny and yet influential component tied to the mighty, irrational *mind*.

516. *Reason* may rule the external world, but it is *passion* that rules the individual mind. Therefore, the day to day mind is struggling more with passion than reason.

517. Physically and sensually we live in one of many possible worlds. Further, *mentally we have been influenced by all possible worlds that surround us* only to ensure that each human mind lands in trouble all the time!

518. *Irrationality* is a darkness extending to infinity. The *mind* is a wanderer without knowing the *destination*. *Reason* is often like lamp posts located, here and there, in the darkness. When a mind reaches the lamp post of reason it receives some guidance on how and where to go about; such minds feel themselves as if boosted with *intellect* and proceed further. But the bulk of the minds are not interested to reach the lamp post, hence not capable of receiving guidance from reason. Such minds rely for external sources like *beliefs*, rituals etc., frequently creating *God* to go further. Only very few minds are endowed with *intuition*, an internal direction that the human mind receives directly from nature and these minds don't bother about the lamp post! Hence,

the mind is always hanging on to any one of the three, *reason*, *God and intuition*, and derives comfort and confidence to move on further. Again all the *three* extend only some kind of comfort, contentment and direction to any particular mind to move on; but in the process they seduce the minds not to ask any question about the very *destination*! The poor mind didn't know 'itself as' the very destination.

519. *Wandering mind*: everyone knows that his mind wanders and hence this fact (that a man's *mind* wanders) is taken for granted, without answering the question why the mind wanders. Our consciousness or existence seems to be an effect of the brain's process involving incoming information, memory and a capacity to process the information. Once the information is received, it in fact it is being received continuously, the processor starts to work all the time and produces additional information. This additionally processed information along with incoming information together forms a further back-feed for the processor. Some of the incoming and processed information are stored in the memory permanently. The memory also regularly supplies material for further processing.

The continuous processing of information and production of ideas by brain activity is apparently presented to us as if a mind is wandering. *What actually happens is that a part of the world both visible and invisible simply passes through the physical brain continuously without human volition*. In the process the brain gets stimulated in numerous ways to the external stimuli. This is felt as though the mind actually wandering!

520. *Frequency* is an irreducible object; by perception everything can be reduced to frequency but the frequency itself cannot be reduced any further. Any further reduction would lead to zero; that *zero* necessarily turns out to be *infinity!*

521. If the sin has its origin in the *mind*, then *god* cannot originate from elsewhere!

522. *Curves* are nature's only favoured shapes. One cannot make any shape without a curvature because nature would always ensure a curvature! No one can draw a *straight line* in the real world. That means straight lines are ideal and only *curves* are real.

523. The world is neither *relative* nor *absolute;* it is an endless overlapping of one over other. This is like the repetitive nature of *stupidity* and *intelligence* that occurs in the course of long human history!

524. In *magic* one man knows and the others are blank; with *mystery, nature* makes that one man also blank!

525. *Desire's* might and power over a man is absolute; even for a god to exist a man has to have desire. The very justification for the God lies in the desire of man. Therefore God is a direct creation of human desire.

526. *Desire* is the king, *love* is the queen. Love is created out of one of the most fundamental aspects of mighty desire. The mighty, blunt, blind, rude and crude desire in itself has certain *gentle elements* that are understandable yet cannot be overpowered by reason. It is the manifestation of these gentle elements at certain times and circumstances largely unknown to a man's mind are felt as the love! Therefore a love itself is composed of all the attributes of desire in

a subdued and restrained way plus the gentleness, *the concern for others*. Love is as blind as and as rude as desire, again the 'concern for other' seems to be *nature's big trick* and a man's poor mind is conscious more of love than the desire and the trick planted in it by nature.

527. The *origin of desire* is permanently not known to the human mind. *The mother of everything is desire, whose mother is not known to the man who desires. Desire is a connection between a known destination and an unknown origin.* If a man desires to become a king, he knows very well the destination as king without knowing why he desires so. Another example is the well known *love*; here again the lover is known but love itself is not known!

528. *Science* cannot understand anything below *three;* the observer, the observed and its surroundings. The number three is the starting point of science. However the truth exists at a level less than three!

529. *Science* and *religion* are two different foods made by the same cook, the human mind.

530. Strong desires lead to *mysteries*. For a physicist his strong desire regularly makes him get involved either with experiments or meditation, physics is a mystery. Despite a great musician the music is still a mystery for him. For a man who loves against all odds lady love is a mystery!

531. A man who believes in one or two *mysteries* is a genius. The one who believes in too many mysteries is an ordinary man; for idiots the world is full of mysteries. After all there is no mystery taking place anywhere without the involvement of the concerned human mind.

532. *Mystery* is born when a human mind accepts its inability and is forced to prematurely admit to the dictates of nature. At this juncture the mighty and blind nature shows man that he is also blind; it happens to everybody, for idiots it happens more frequently than others.

533. The majority of *nature* is blind more to a man's eyes than to his mind. Hence a mind is able to understand more than what the senses can disclose.

534. *God* is a blind man's beautiful creation.

535. *God*, *love* and *justice*: are progressive stages of the human mind in that order.

536. *Love* is supported by nature, while social circumstances, passion and a bit of reason support *friendship*. *Nature* is never a source of *friendship*!

537. In general, the source of *friendship* lies in the mind that begins to understand the idea of *equality*. But the very idea of equality is *often* dictated by *circumstances* rather than *reason*.

538. A man's mind, however big it may be, is only partial and a woman mind, however small it may be, is *almost* complete. A *man's* destination is *woman*, but women are destinations by themselves!

539. The world has only one wonder: it is neither god nor ghost nor the drifting of galaxies nor even the existence of a black hole or any other kind of wild imagination possible, but rather it is man's *mind*.

540. *Economic progress* happens when the mind attempts to transfer physical pain to mental pain. While the body has very limited capacity to venture further, the mind plunges

into action betting on its nearly unlimited capacity; it all works but only at the cost of a serious mind-body mismatch.

541. The only grace of *democracy* is that everybody will get his chance, however small or bad it may be!

542. *Culture* is a big shield created by society against nature; yet *nature* punctures the shield as often as possible with the connivance of individuals who made the shield!

543. *Life* is more of a feeling and a crude awareness than *logic* and *reason.* Feeling is fundamental to life. If logic does not understand the reason behind the feeling and the fundamental nature of it, it has no practical worth and hence cannot save men from misery.

544. *Reason* says *life* has no purpose but as an accident. If life is an accident then reason itself came into existence only out the same accident. A leaf cannot question the existence of a branch and the branch cannot question the existence the trunk. Life's purpose exists in the very nature of life itself.

545. *Existence* is not questionable since the one that questions is already in existence.

546. *The mind* is at war with nature on one side and peace on other side only due to the acts of human reason. The war will end only when *reason* is suppressed. However, if reason is suppressed he is no more a human!

547. *The mind* has no distance; only senses impose distance on the *human mind* and force the mind to create *time*!

548. *Fear* is an awareness of certainty about uncertainty. *Death* is the master fear and hence resides at the top of

'all other fears'. In the case of that master fear, death, the event is known to happen for certain but the *time* is not known; in case of all other fears time is known but the result is not known!

549. *Uncertainty is the motivating force behind a man's mind.* It is the very awareness and understanding of uncertainty that forces the mind to create an order in the world of disorder. It makes mind to travel back and forth to engage itself in worldly affairs, instigates and coerces a mind to the extent of creating god to manage exigencies and contingent needs etc. *Uncertainty* is not a threat on the other hand it makes the mind *creative*! *Certainty is of no use, when everything is certain there is no mind; certainty dissolves the human mind!*

550. *Uncertainty* is the first, the last and the only lesson that *nature* teaches a man.

551. When *nature* throws *uncertainty* at man, the best possible reaction is when the man throws a *god* at the nature! This way only god got stuck between man and nature.

552. Resigning to one's *fate* is the simplest form of *enlightenment*!

553. *Rotation* is the basic, primary nature of worldly objects. *Revolution* is derived and hence the secondary nature of things. Revolution is an after effect of rotation and hence the former is organically connected to the latter; all kinds of motions are finally linked to the underlying primary rotation only.

554. *Intelligence* is like the water in a stream; but the stream itself is knowledge. Intelligence is often limited and has no element within it to regulate itself. The *knowledge* as

a stream with its bed and banks guides the intelligence. Sometimes the intelligence, like water, dries up but nothing happens to the banks hence the knowledge. Intelligence is part of knowledge, but need not be a necessary part.

555. *Intelligence* exists in a closed room; *knowledge* is born when windows are opened.

556. The *truth* is a bare fact enacted by nature. Therefore it exists without any particular perspective until a human mind imposes its own perspective on the truth, like the good and bad.

557. Human beings are left with only these two options: either create *god* or fight with *reason*. The former is the easier than the latter and hence becomes the most preferred choice.

558. It is a fact that *fools* sleep more peacefully than the *intelligent*; but every time they wake up only as fools!

559. To achieve something *great* in life one should have a strong *desire* or at least one *tragedy*! *Intelligence* comes a distant third.

560. The problem with *intelligence* is its entanglement with 'parts' while *knowledge* begins from the whole.

561. *Lies* have its own role due to its usefulness in society. But it is *democracy* that acts as a breeding ground for all possible kinds of lies. It is the false freedom and the carefully crafted lies that sustain a democracy.

562. *Religion* is for the individual, whilst *reason* is for the state and *morality* is for both.

563. *Culture* is born out of men's intentions to modify nature and hence to that extent it is 'naturally' deceitful.

564. *Science* is a lie in daylight, in fact with a lot of witnesses. *Religion* is a truth in darkness, obviously without the need for any such witnesses! *Science* is partial but bright. *Religion* is whole but dark. Every *religious claim* has been proved wrong and every *scientific truth* has been verified as inadequate. That is the way they work, as religion relies on the inherent weakness of human minds and science survives on only its *present* ability to satisfy reason with its inherently approximate nature of observations and subsequent proofs based on it. Therefore, *yesterday's religious claims never become* the *truth today and today's scientific truths never turn out to be real claims tomorrow!*

565. Any *useful lie is* glorified more than the truth only because of its usefulness! As time progresses these useful lies become mainstream practical *truths*, as none feels it as a lie.

566. If everyone is made out to be bad, later it will be feasible for everyone to claim that they are good also! The latent aim of *democracy* is to create such an atmosphere so that every human nature tacitly agrees to that idea!

567. If *ignorance* is a sin, then some other men *living* on *that* ignorance is a sin of the sin.

568. *Status*, *power* and *wealth* only aid and amplify the underlying basic human instincts.

569. *Patience* is the teacher of teachers; understanding one's own '*wild nature*' is the first step towards enlightenment.

570. *The rational and irrational acts*: in case of *rational acts* the deciding forces are known to the human mind, but

the *irrational acts owe* their origin to unknown forces. Just because the forces are unknown do not automatically downgrade the importance of irrational acts. In the day to day world a human mind is ruled by irrational forces with *reason* often being a mute witness. Reason is clever to know this and hence create enough reasons to act against the irrational nature of the mind either to protect man or at least misguide at sometimes, but at all other times reason does not know the reasons why it failed to act. *The fate of reason is to evolve since nature never teaches the full lesson to reason!*

571. Despite being intelligent, strong and courageous *reason is only an adopted son of nature;* despite being stupid and blind *faith* is the natural son of the nature!

572. A *single man* is irrational. *Reason* is born only out of social interaction.

573. *Immortality* is ultimate limit of fear on one side and self-glorification on the other.

574. Originally *nature* frightened man, hence first he become *fearful* before becoming *social*. Again, the original fear never vanished but it started getting gradually accumulated in the subconscious mind despite the evolution and also due to the very evolution! This accumulated fear and added confusion happened during the formation of society which ultimately led to the birth of religion. Hence the chronology is: *fear*, *confusion*, *society* and *religion*.

575. It is fine, impeccable and subtle nature of a *woman's mind* that imparts them with the capacity to survive in adverse circumstances which a *man* cannot often imagine. An

average *man's mind* is largely derived, coarse, widespread, shallow and uselessly strong in comparison to a woman's. In fact the existence of women very often proves that the subtle are stronger than the strong!

576. No *enlightenment* is possible without conquering *reason*. Reason itself is not a part of enlightenment but it is a pathway to be traversed; it aids and provides a *checklist* that has to be either validated or disproved before leading to anything like enlightenment. A weak and stupid mind sidetracks reason out of fear and madness. Therefore no real enlightenment is achievable without reason, as it is a conscious process. If enlightenment is possible without reason, then all animals, birds and worms would already be enlightened!

577. *Eye* is the index of heart.

578. The creation of *God* is a voluntary attempt to stop an endless mental process born out of fear and uncertainty that a man often encounters. God is like a safety valve beyond which *mind* does not want to cook food any more.

579. If life is an accident, the 'human' *mind* is an *accident* within the accident. Then, the reason is the grandson of the first accident!

580. If a man alone is introspected he would appear as an *accident* of nature; if a woman is understood alongside a man there would emerge some *purpose*! But if eunuchs are included for examination again accidental nature would prevail. Therefore *existence* of accident never disallows the existence of *purpose;* it all depends from what perspective and up to what range the mind is capable of looking and interpreting the nature around.

581. *Intelligent man* will never be the first one to take a *risk*.

582. How *nature* works is not known to us, but there is a vital clue: *instinct*. I strongly believe that nature works through *instinct*. Instinct is something within us yet for all practical purposes it is not within our control. A man cannot dictate instinct that is connected to the large unknown; instead he invents *god*, only to *meddle* with the instincts in the ways favourable to him, and thus god is made to exist between man and nature.

583. *The mind* reflects the state of existence of all other things, while *God* reflects the state of human mind.

584. *God exists between man and nature*; but man often bypasses and colludes with nature.

585. *Infinity* and *zero*: the world has *infinite* things. If all the things are added, the result will become *zero*. To verify this fact one has to simply close his eyes, and of course the other senses too.

586. *Reason*: at various stages in human life, the one that is glorified, subdued, tamed, abused, chased away and often recalled with respect is *reason!*

587. *Reason* is a master for the youth. It is an admirable *friend* among progressive young men. The same reason's status is relegated to a servant in wealthy and powerful men's household. In the final scenes of a matured man's life reason is gradually overlooked, ignored and dumped unheeded by the mind only to join hands with the irrational *nature*.

588. *Imagination* is not possible, if mind has no *intention* to possess the facts and events; but imagination manifests

explicitly in the form of human actions but hardly the intention!

589. If the physical world is probed from coarser material things towards finer and finer things that actually makes us move from *sense* based experimentation to a *mind* based belief system; such inquiry and subsequent understanding makes our mind travel from science to religion; the sooner the mind seems to be an extension of material. But if we start from mind then all material objects seem to be creation of mind with help of human senses. One way the mind seems to be as an extension of material and the other way it creates all material objects. This contradiction can be avoided only if mind represents all of the material things and vice-versa. From the perspective of human beings, during the initial stages mind develops and grows with the help of senses, but finally to behave like an independent authority. *A mind first studies in a school set up by the senses only to become the teacher of the school!*

590. *Art* is a child born to the father called *memory* and mother called *imagination*.

591. *Virtue* was adorned even during ancient times; accordingly it was *scarce* since the very beginning!

592. *Art* exists in the deepest location of a shallow mind!

593. During scarcity, *beauty* is a product of circumstances; while in abundance the same is born out of a choice.

594. Individual *skills* are the result of the randomness of nature, the basic criterion for formation of society; order never creates order!

595. The domination of the human *instinct* and subsequent awareness of uncertainties make the very definition of *morality* difficult, leave alone the practice of it.

596. There may be many religions; but *nature is the supreme religion of religions*. Nature dictates to religion more often than religion does the same to a man.

597. *Nature* as a body has *uncertainty* and *randomness* as its two legs for mobility.

598. The awareness of *fear of death* precedes both god and spiritualism. A man's life is either consciously or unconsciously, a continuous attempt to reconcile to this single fact. One man constructs a story saying everything has a 'purpose' while the other argues that things are happening only by chance, but both the stories thrive on and around the single underlying fact: the certainty of *death*.

599. A man gives meaning to birth only after he becomes aware of his *death*; until then *birth* had no meaning. His *mind* cannot glorify death until it tactfully decides to infuse a purpose in birth itself. The poor mind does all these tricks only to overcome the frailties of its own existence. The mind is an expert in making something meaningful after it becomes fully aware of its meaningless nature!

600. All the activities however wisely and tactfully a mind undertakes to escape from the *hard fact* are in fact nothing but preparation in disguise to face the same inevitable hard fact, *death*.

601. *Death*: The awareness of *death* despairs an intelligent man, threatens and transforms a foolish man. The former

does not realize that his intelligence is only with respect to another man not with respect to *nature* and the latter somehow orients him-self along nature! The great *nature* is stupidest of all; it cannot understand the amusing ways in which a human *mind* works.

602. Whatever the *mind* creates is *good* for it, because it became a necessity only from equally *bad* mental conditions; a good buds either from the awareness or from the experience of bad, therefore it never exists independently!

603. Nature troubles the human *mind* through the *body* and the mind tortures the body in the name of culture; at any instance practically both are never out of trouble.

604. *Nature and Reason:* reason in its strong and capable phase during a human life discovers more questions than its own ability to get answers. Hence, it looks towards *nature* for answers. Nature being a master dictator, never fully heeds to reason but resorts to providing second rate answers. Reason with all its might and valour has only to settle for whatever it is able get; interestingly reason claims these acts as its great achievements and resigns to fate only to understand later that nature has tricked them. But the untiring reason again raises questions, this time more intelligent than earlier, only to meet the same fate later. Reason is always in a hurry but never able to meddle with the way and the rate at which nature unfolds itself.

605. In the world of practice a man is more concerned about truth, existence etc., but a woman adapts herself to natural ways and thus makes these issues hardly have any practical consequence on her.

606. Again the *nature and reason*: *reason* is able to help, with its various ideas like *essence*, *existence*, *beginning*, *end*, *time* etc., to manufacture the most intelligent questions that are not fully answered by Nature. Reason cannot blame nature because the latter is irrational. What reason trumpets as *vital questions* are actually an unreasonable excess and are never heeded by nature. Reason is always searching for 'essence' or 'beginning' only with its limited capacity of senses and hence it understands the physical world despite the superior manipulative power of mind. But this is nothing to despair, by not providing the clues and not allowing it to reach the final destination, nature ensures a continuous progress of reason; otherwise reason has no further work to do. Reason occurs to man only as an evolutionary component and as such its usefulness is with respect to the nature immediately surrounding him.

607. A *man* who does not want anything is already owner of everything!

608. *Great men* don't worry about the good and bad ascribed to them by others, but definitely concerned about their own resolute conscience.

609. *The human existence and the limit of reason*: to understand reason we have no one for our assistance but the very *reason!* Human reason says that animals have no reason like man. This may be because all men believe that no animals would have troubled minds like us! In other words the animals are more close to nature than human beings and with a reason.

It is beyond doubt that the reason does wonders with the help of the limited numbers of instruments called the human senses, but all up to a certain limit or range. The limitation happens not only due to the limited numbers of senses, but due to the limited capacity of each sense. Reason manipulates the information provided by the senses to some extent, say to a reasonable extent, and understands the nature to its 'own' satisfaction; again only to its own satisfaction.

However the same reason is not able assist us in vital issues like its own *existence* beyond the certain limit, may be understood as a 'reasonable limit'. As such *existence* is really beyond examination! By only examining a limited part of the visible world, reason becomes ambitious and tries to understand the essence of existence; it does so unsuccessfully.

In fact many religions deal with the issue of existence much *better* than reason. However even a religion can only be better than reason in regard to this particular issue, *existence*, *without* actually showing the way. This is because religious experiences are subjective; the very subjectivity makes the existence *indeterminate*, not really understandable. *Nature*, the blind master, only laughs at reason, because there is nothing called essence or existence or essence of existence from nature's perspective. In fact the *blind fellow* has no perspective at all! Yet reason knocks on the door of the blind man house repeatedly and expects an explanation from him. The blind master appreciates the hard work of reason but he does not know how to help the anxious student.

The real problem is, *the blind master can only teach during the 'night' and the young man is only capable of learning during the 'day'. Blind nature is like a black hole while reason is like a bright star waiting to be sucked.*

Reason has no escape except to change its own nature; reason transforms itself and abandons its idea of proof to reconcile with the issue of *existence*. This way reason transforms itself as blind; after such a changeover the same reason takes a new avatar in the form of *faith*. Now the situation becomes blind verses blind and hence the necessary compatibility. Faith being blind, blindly believes in *nature*! Faith never troubles nature with questions relating to either the essence or existence as reason did earlier. Faith is not at all worried about questions and answers; it does not want to even become aware of such questions. The job of faith is to ensure peace and harmony; hence it effortlessly surrenders to the master nature to save a conscious human being from the exigencies.

In brief 'reason' is not able to prove existence in any objective way and hence transforms itself as faith in favour of a subjective experience; the latter is better than the *former since at least one man is experiencing something himself despite not being able to convince others with his experience. Again reason without objectivity and faith only with subjectivity makes any existence including 'human existence' only as indeterminate. Thus neither the fighting reason nor the surrendering faith solved the issue of existence. Therefore a human existence is fundamentally indeterminate!*

610. *Confusion* is a pre-requisite for a human *mind* to progress.

611. The belief in *essence and its existence* together with *time* forms a closed boundary with fencing within which the *reason* has to work. However, while roaming within this finite territory clever reason often wants to have

close look at the very boundary; it desires to verify what the boundary itself consists of since it believes in the existence of such boundary. When it nears the boundary for a close gaze, it is not able to see the fencing because it needs adequate distance to observe; each time it nears the boundary the fencing moves away making it available only for a distant look and thus forever avoiding a close-up view to the eyes of reason. The moving boundary definitely makes reason despair but in the process its territory gets expanded and that turned out to be real a consolation for reason!

612. *God* has been made a '*standing justification*' for the existence of a man and all kinds of his activities. God is the mind's way of controlling and regulating itself.

613. The world broadly has only two types of *idiots*: those that believe in god and those who do not believe in god! Atheists don't want to understand mind due to reason and its aide, science. Theists always misunderstand the mind due to the comfort and convenience rendered by blind belief. *The mind is either misused or disused whenever the question of god is involved.*

614. *Reason* and *time*: In general both invariably have an agreeable and significant working alliance; time always comforts and guides reason to decide what human action to be and advice how an action is relevant for that particular brief period of *time* only. But in course of time reason either becomes cunning or violates the counsel of the time! Reason always has an ambition to go for the excess, even if it gets the slightest opportunity; this way *reason* often desires to sit in judgment by conveniently forgetting the existence of *time*. Reason musters enough

strength and determination only to think that it has unlimited competency to decide once and for all on the issues of nature or social, religious etc.,

In brief reason aims at delivering a *timeless* judgment, one that is enduring and not affected by the passage of time. Therefore reason subsequently decides to dump and break the alliance with *time;* by the time reason dumps, time switches its loyalty to the *mind!* Every time mind creates new time and hence new justification is born jeopardizing the reason's towering ambitions to create a timeless judgment.

Finally *the intelligent and indomitable reason loses to a stupid human mind due to its own unreasonable excess; time favours the mind to win. Time is a great friend of reason however if the latter ditches, the former teaches, a lesson by invalidating and damaging the judgments of human reason.*

615. The *human mind* is an effect. *Time* is an effect of that effect.

616. All *bad* things are causes and therefore all *good* things are effects!

617. *Nature* has no time.

618. *Time is never born until eyes are opened, a hand touches another object, a nose smells the scent.* When the mind operates the human senses the continuous world becomes a discontinuous world with numerous discrete entities. The senses provide only static information but the mind has the intention to store information. In this process born are the time and memory both simultaneously.

Therefore *time is a by-product of* the *mental process*, obviously subjective and specific to that mind without any independent existence. Therefore, without the operation of senses the world is always continuous and hence *time* is not a possibility. Hence, *time is never born until the eyes are opened!*

619. *Time* helps to understand everything. But time itself is not comprehensible, since it would again require *time*!

620. However *good* he may be, a 'small man' is only small. However *bad* he may be, a 'big man' remains big only! Good is always good however small he may be and bad is always bad however big he may be!

621. *Faith* does not require time!

622. *Time* is the best friend of *reason*. But often reason is not so with time!

623. From the perspective of the *reason*, *time* is like a knife. Reason uses the 'time' to cut nature in its attempt to understand it. But reason never knows how to stitch it; it becomes the job of *faith*.

624. Ultimately a *man* turns out to be as stupid as his *nature*.

625. *Reason* is interested only in physical objects; the only 'metal object' it supports and befriends is *time*. Reason has a capacity to question and ill-treat all other mental objects, like faith, morality, good, bad, virtue, including *god* etc. up to a limit where its own purpose and existence becomes questionable by *time*. Ultimately, it *is time that shows the limit of the young warrior, the reason.*

626. *Science* and *religion* will have to always co-exist the same way as body and mind co-exists together but for the

narrow comprehensive power of certain minds. When body and mind function so amicably, there is no reason for science and religion to be antagonistic to each other. Science is often dry and not bothered about human emotions only to make the mind crazy and hence rituals and religion.

627. If one *fact* replaces another it is *science* and if one *story* replaces another it is called *religion*.

628. The *mind* creates god only to use in the event of trouble and at all other times to misuse. After all food is beneficial only when a man is in hunger.

629. The mind is a restless creator of stories. The compilation of all such extensive 'off the ground' stories came to be known as *religion* in all societies and the hero of the story always turned out to be *god*. It is amusing to see that the content of the story changes continuously but not the *title*. Nature of the hero changes but not the name of hero! This is because the creators of the story change but the stories never stop!

630. Reason aims for human understanding and *meaning* in each and every thing and faith is worried about *existence* and survival. *When the existence becomes more meaningful than meaning full existence, the faith overtakes reason*!

631. In love, *romance* is the transition from *culture* towards *nature*. It is a mutually acceptable intermediate stage set by culture on one side and nature on the other, before nature calls the final shots!

632. In every misfortune *man* goes to *god*, in every fortune either he forgets god or claims himself as god.

633. Basic *misery* is always present in the mind, some are aware and some do not. Among those who are aware some overcome it and others do not. The power, money, celebrity and status do not positively help overcome the misery; however they work in different way: enable a mind to over look its own misery by looking at other man's misery!

634. The *mind* is a stupid master; it mindlessly believes the even stupider servants, the senses.

635. If a man really wants to *help* someone, then he should not listen to that someone!

636. At first, say in childhood, the *mind* is really excited about everything because all are *unknown* things and surroundings waiting to be *known*. As a man grows up knowing the things of nature fascinates and interests him. Gradually, as the time progresses the mind loses interest in the things that it comes to understand better and better; in the process of knowing the mind accumulates more unknown stuff than the known. The mind by frequently working on this way starts building a favourable opinion about the unknown than the known. Hence, at the start and end the mind is more attached to the unknown than the known; only in the intervening period the mind is taken for a detour where *reason* rules the roost.

637. *Science* starts with matter; the very existence of *matter* is taken for granted, on the matter subsequently the facts and theories have been built. Science is never able to describe what the matter itself is composed of due to the limitations imposed by the senses. In the world of the senses one cannot deny the existence of matter, since the very same senses are also assumed to be made up of

the matter. Exactly the same thing happens in *religion*, instead of matter, the *mind* is taken for granted. All religions, without seeking to know how and why mind exist, construct stories and rituals to satisfy the feelings and inclinations of the mind just as science does to validate the matter.

In short, what science does with *matter* and its properties religion does with the mind and its *feelings*. Both science and religion function in identical ways and hence the preference of one over the other is more due to individual mental preference, inclination and comfort than any other fundamental basis.

638. If an action does not contradict one's own *conscience*, then it can be justified as *dharma*. By dharma, more than anything else, a man at least has the sanction of his conscience, the subtle yet accessible one.

639. *Senses* are as mechanical as a car; a *mind* is analogous to the driver. The driver only knows the destination and hence sets the direction of car accordingly. But without the car the driver himself is jobless!

640. *Beauty* is produced by biology and judged by sociology. In order to validate *evolution*, today's biology has to the result of yesterday's sociology.

641. *Morality* is a thin wall between *reason* and *passion*. The wall is so thin that passion demolishes it as often as feasible while reason rebuilds it as quickly as possible.

642. By *art*, a man has already lost the reality of things and events.

643. The *matter* is given by senses and hence matter becomes the pre-requisite for science, similarly the *self* becomes so

for religion. In fact, the former as the basis for science and the latter for religion is taken for granted without any need for proof! To that extent both are questionable, but there is no escape route. The inescapability from both only made them the two great pillars of human civilization. Without matter, science would perish; a religion that denies the *self* will only create its own contradictions. In order to overcome these contradictions the same religion has to subsequently create more stories than what was told to us originally!

644. *Truth* and *falsehood* are human interpretations of nature. But *good* and *bad* are judgments of society and come to be nothing more than local cultural yardsticks. However the impact of them on the human mind is so tremendous that in the course of time they become ingrained in the biology of human beings that finally lead to the advent of *morality*. Therefore morality is local yet it has a long history, that history only imparts an authority to it.

645. *Nature* cheats every human mind. *Reason* whether able to stop it or not definitely makes us 'aware' of it. But the beauty of *religion* lies in its *lies;* the beautiful lies have the ability to turn us away from the very awareness of it!

646. *Nature* is a big liar. We, sitting within nature, are not even its faithful followers often forced to speak some truth!

647. It is obvious that *power* and *wealth* are less to do with common sense. However, in comparison, powerful men are less stupid than their wealthier counterparts. Again power does more harm to others while wealth does the same to its possessor!

648. The progress of *civilization* distorts the *mind*; survival becomes more difficult due the resulting confusion and

uncertainty. A mind generates more questions than answers and hence it is not able to manage by itself. This finally forces the vulnerable minds to gullible pseudo sages who meditate every day and fabricate soothing stories as answers to the naive and stupid questions of defenceless minds.

649. For purely *mental* purposes, *existence* and *non-existence* are neither contradictory nor something fundamentally different issues!

650. As the world becomes *real* and real, the concerned human mind becomes *ideal*.

651. A *woman's mind* is can be easily trained than that of man. This is because either a man or a rational society only can mislead a woman but in that process her mind hardly gets distorted. Nature restores a woman's mind to its original state more easily than the distorted, deformed and disoriented mind of a man.

652. If a *beautiful woman* is to remain beautiful after twenty years his original aesthetics sense is excellent, but his fate is fixed.

653. The *world* was always same: it was neither *good* today nor *bad* yesterday or vice versa. But individual minds have limited ability or circumstances restricted them to grasp only some aspects and details of world of today. Again they came to know and compare only some similar yet faint aspects in the past to the issues of present more familiar issues and arrive at a decision, the *good* or *bad*. Such innumerable individual minds by benchmarking only on the scant knowledge of the present and still obscure and distorted information of the past

conveniently came to a conclusion that the world today is better or worse compared to yesterday.

654. *Individual freedom* is not possible without understanding nature; again nature is not waiting there for anybody to understand it.

655. *Life* is a fine balance between *expectation* and *reconciliation* but often both happen simultaneously!

656. *Reason* fools, especially young men, by promising *objectivity*. Reason makes *perception* as the starting point of any understanding; perception being a sense based activity, accordingly a man is able perceive whatever is outside of him, while that perceives is actually sitting inside of him which he is not able to perceive! This way the mighty reason's flamboyant claims based on perception is partial and one-sided.

But there is a *higher faculty* within him that reminds him about the existence of the connection between the perceived and what perceives, and also that has not been able to be perceived by senses. *Reason*, with its trusted associate called *science*, either by severing the connection or being indifferent to it creates only an '*agreed upon objectivity*' for a limited purpose of satisfying the curiosity of the mind that arises in relation the surrounding physical world. Reason with the assistance of science created specific laws and predetermined rules look at the things in a restricted way and claims an *objectivity* only in the background of these presupposed rules while the things by themselves are not existing objectively; *something* is objective only for that particular perspective not otherwise. The same thing can again be objective, in a different way, for a different set of pre-established rules and laws. *Existence of such different objectivities for the same thing logically makes the entire situation subjective! The sum of objectivities led to a conclusively subjective view; hence any objectivity by itself is only some part of a largely subjective thing.*

Therefore reason and science do not provide absolute objectivity worth pursuing for the purpose of understanding nature in relation to his own nature, but definitely a limited yet useful one; it is strange that reason directs a human mind to understand *others,* while by itself cannot understand the same mind; *science is an 'agreed upon objectivity' nothing more and nothing less. Hence science is an approximation of the real, religion is a feeling of real and an art is a distorted feeling of real.* In fact all these *three* are actually *subjective*.

However science is intelligent enough to make the *subjectivity* acceptable to a larger section of people. This because science stares at physical world only within its perspective of predetermined and already established laws. As such within these 'agreed upon' premises only the really *subjective* turned out to be *objective*, for science. The *agreed upon* rules enables science to create itself a universal language to be communicated to its members, while art and religion do not and also cannot do so with *mental feeling* as their central theme.

Strangely, *science on one hand escaped from subjectivity by not including the mind as within its ambit of study, on the other it went on to claim objectivity only with the help of the same mind!*

657. What *religion* does with some people, *reason* does with some other people; a man always left in a wilderness by nature has no other choices!

658. The world within him is decided by *intentions* and outside is by *words*; any man who is able to match his intentions with words can rightly claim the post of *god*.

659. A bad man can tell a lot of good stories; but a good man really has no story to tell, if he does so it will only be a bad story! *After all each man is a story; and stories are an integral part of any civilized society.*

660. A man who overreacts has already decided to hide something.

661. If public *memory* is intact no man can become *holy*; if a man's own memory is intact he will not claim himself as holy!

662. *Nature* is effective, but perceived as imperfect! Natural objects move because of this imperfection. All creations become a possibility only due to this imperfect motion; again all these are from a human perspective; then, where do men search for perfection!

663. *Nature* never laid any yardstick for perfection, but *man*. Only the human mind makes its own yardstick and claims it as *perfection;* and also works towards it as if it is real!

664. *Perfection* itself is a template of imperfection created by the mind within itself. But that template is much better than any of the existing things that it intends to understand. Mind does that every time. Why should the mind create such an imperfect template every time? This is because the mind tries to understand the nature by always starting somewhere in-between while nature being

continuous; from the starting point it has to necessarily move on, that is the inherent property of the mind. For any motion to take place the mind needs a direction while nature is not ready to show any direction. Hence the mind itself has to create its own direction by taking a cue from the starting point. The starting point is in the physical world. Hence, it treats whatever it knows about the starting point as imperfect and rudimentary and aims to proceed to an improved level that is not available anywhere in the physical world. Hence, the mind creates a template of an improved level than the starting point and believes it as perfection and moves on and on.

665. By *love* a man wants to be useful to first himself and then from this strong primary instinct, a man's rest of the world is derived.

666. Human reason has an ability to create mentally good things, yet strangely it is incapable of owning them; hence all such good things get independence as soon as they are created. Thereafter inept reason is only left with longing for its own creations!

667. At one extreme man is at the mercy of *circumstances* totally external to him and at the other he is being destroyed by *reason*. A man's life is the sum total of all his attempts to escape from either of these two.

668. *Belief and superstition*: within the radius of *stupidity* any belief is not only immensely useful but also indistinguishable from it! *Superstition* always roams closer to the centre of the circle.

669. When a man consciously *forgoes* something then that something roams around indifferent avatars to serve

him; instead if he tries hard to possess it, it troubles and torments him.

670. A man who is afraid of the *truth* becomes a slave of everything.

671. My dear *reason*, do not strangle the mind too much after all you are always attached to it!

672. An *absence* of something is also its *presence*, because it has an effect to that extent!

673. There is a *limit* up to which *reason* is able to guide or protect a man. However, beyond this limit even if the reason tries to direct him, his conscience destroys his own inner strength; if reason is not able to change his actions he is already in the hands of his *fate*! *Where the jurisdiction of reason ends there starts the jurisdiction of fate.* Even in the region of fate there definitely exists reason but as a spectator! Still worse it makes a man *aware* of what he cannot handle. Therefore the human mind slowly brings in a *belief* either to kill or divert the very awareness.

674. In general, an atheist misses so many subtle things to claim that there is no god and a theist adds so many contradictions to claim there is a god! God is not an explanation but rather for he or she it is a *net* feeling whose origin is as deep and subtle as the concerned man's own existence.

675. Each *woman* is a world in herself; *men* reside only in the overlapping regions!

676. *Fate* plays a big role in an ordinary man's life because his mind is not able to become big enough. A big man is

always the captive of his fate because he does not want to become a small man!

677. It is not due to *reason* that a man *desires* to do something; instead it is the other way around. Reason is always second fiddle to human desire.

678. *Conscience and god*: when the human mind lacks conscience or intends to go against its own conscience a god is made to act as a defence mechanism of that mind; this way conscience becomes above god. Human history is a standing witness to the transformation that happens in the nature of both the *god* and *conscience*. The adjustments in conscience become a necessity to be in tune with nature and culture while the similar correction in god has to happen to satisfy a human conscience!

679. The *truth* and *falsehood* are irrational and primary. The *good* and *bad* are a bit more rational yet local and secondary.

680. A man's reason surrendering to his own nature is called *fate*!

681. Science is built on *matter* while religion is built on *misery*; as such both are resting on the unknown!

682. Spiritualism is a *feeling*; however sacred or stupid it may be, the end product of human existence is nothing more than a feeling either of happiness or melancholy.

683. A man's ultimate destination is not *god* but *peace*; the god is being used only as an intended mean to achieve certain purposes, while the ultimate purpose is peace.

684. A *leader's* intention starts and ends within himself; leadership never assumes the involvement of followers.

Hence a man who intends to collect a group of men cannot be the true leader. A man who behaves for the sake of others is actually a follower or a dupe!

685. *Self-respect* is a culmination of inner strength supported by reason; when reason collapses the self- respect evaporates.

686. Whatever helps a man regulate his mind becomes part of his *religion*. The man who cannot change his mind starts justifying its actions. If he does so repeatedly such actions become capable of regulating him. Whatever regulates a mind also has its origin in the mind itself, therefore the *god*.

687. The mind does the job of *creation*; reason just *names* and justifies it whenever required!

688. One day there will not be any *nationalism*; science and technology will kill the emotions based on geography only to start new groups and divisions based on virtual feelings.

689. *Communism* is a fancy of immaturity where rogues overpower human sensibility. *Capitalism* is an idiot's pleasure where the body overwhelms the mind; the amoral combination of *democracy* and capitalism makes greater opportunities available to animals than to the scientists.

690. *Fear* has a thousand incarnations and *belief* is the most sacred one out of all.

691. Even today all religions are more or less same because *men* are still afraid of *women*!

692. A man who evades his *conscience* is a dupe. An *original* man always aligns with his conscience.

693. *God* is the biggest confusion even the smallest human mind can ever make before finally settling down to its own world of prejudices!

694. *Fate* is a path that *reason* repeatedly failed to avoid. The reason for failure is not known since the reason only failed! Yet, the failure probably might be either due to weakness of the reason or due to strong instinct!

695. The *fear* destroys whatever little meaning a life has.

696. *God* is everyone's pleasure and also everyone's prejudice!

697. A man thinks another man is *good* only to find the latter to be *bad* someday for sure. But in a similar way who he thinks as bad doesn't become good some other day then the man always assumes himself to be good!

698. A *business* is a malleable coin of which one side is *survival* and the other side is *cheating*. The thin edge, often too thin, joining both these sides is *claimed* as social service. As the business progresses the sides of the malleable coin become flatter and flatter at the expense of the already thin edge!

699. I am too small, yet the world outside me is still smaller than my *conscience*!

700. Fate never affects a man of *conscience* because he is already travelling with it! He knows the *rate* of the fate because he already paid the price!!

701. If all the politicians of world do not use their brains for *few days*, the world will be more peaceful and governance should become easier by at least five times. If all scientists stop experimenting for 'few years' then nature will be more natural, as it is less disturbed. If all the *women* do

not talk only *for moments*, the disturbance to the earth's magnetic field would be halved. If all the religious men and women had not demanded anything from god for few days many of them would have already met god. All are really simple and achievable except the third statement!

702. A man cannot really hide anything; whatever he hides emanates from somewhere else whether he knows or not. A man's *intentions* leak all the time!

703. The combination of the mind, reason and senses is such that what is clearly perceived and defined by *reason* doesn't exist; whatever cannot be defined so, certainly exists!

704. When knowledge becomes stagnant a man becomes *expert*, otherwise intelligent!

705. When the world around a man is stupid it elevates him fast, only to make him feel intelligent compared to the rest but when the same world emerges as intelligent he soon falls steeper again only to feel his *stupidity* even better than earlier. His latter stupidity makes him more enlightened than his former intelligence.

706. The one who lacks *reason* cheats him-self repeatedly; others don't cheat him but the inadequacy of reason makes him available for others.

707. When a man thinks about something, it starts to exist in his mind; when he believes the same it starts influencing him. This is the way a god or a ghost for that man came into existence. But the question, '*why*' he started *thinking* and subsequently *believing* in that something is far more subtle and important than '*what*' he thought and believed!

708. *God* naturally reaches out to those fearful and stupid. Those who are intelligent logically reach out to god. For all those 'in-between' the god becomes an on and off issue involving frequent confusion!

709. A man who keeps quiet finds the shortest route to the *truth*. But truth itself finds the shortest time to reach a man of *patience*.

710. A man who is afraid of his own *mind* takes shelter under money, power and status etc.; otherwise the reverse happens.

711. *Life* has endless definitions brought throughout the very life process.

712. The human being is the only creature that is stupid enough to feel as an *intelligent* and intelligent enough to understand its *stupidity*.

713. When a world created by a man wanes what is visible is the *truth*, the world that created the man!

714. A man's *intelligence* is always with reference to yesterday; he is stupid if the reference becomes tomorrow. Hence anybody's knowledge at *any instance* has two sides though he is expected to project only the favourable side.

715. *Intelligence* is continuously built on stupidity and *good* is built on bad; this process is being called knowledge.

716. It is very much possible for intelligence, honesty and *perversion* to coexist; the third ingredient makes one utterly selfish in social relations despite the fact that the first two indirectly contribute to society.

717. *Fate*, *dharma*, *karma* or any other thing however great they may be, if a man understands they are within him otherwise he is within them.

718. *Science* has every raw material except the mind to prove that the *first god* is the one that created man, but reason prevents it. Religion has no hard evidence yet makes a man propose the second god, the one man created.

719. *Strife* is an inevitable event that has happen before *peace*. Peace cannot be achieved without adequate learning process; strife imparts a lot of knowledge even to a stupid person. Therefore the 'stupid majority' would never grasp the meaning of peace unless strife is passed over.

720. *A real life*: if a man and woman live together a scuffle, altercations, skirmish and subsequent reconciliation all help improve their *prudence*; but if they separate and live alone then they end up with improved *reason*. The prudence is practical, natural and has an ability to inherently take care of emotions. The reason is sound, dispassionate and makes one to judge better yet it is dry. *Human life is predominately a natural process involving more of adjustments than judgments. Hence on practical matters it is prudent to develop prudence by reasonably passing over the reason!*

721. *Lies* always have a purpose; but a *truth* has no such compulsion! *The very purpose of lies is that they have to be told somewhere; otherwise there arises no necessity to create them*. The truth exists as it is; only some confess and others do not.

722. *Villains* have lesser nerves than *heroes*. Villain has numerically less but strong ones. However, the hero has numerous and well-graded ones and that make him adaptable to many more circumstances. In short, a villain can trouble a hero only in limited ways while the hero 'potentially' has many more ways to escape!

723. In the world of human beings, only the *good* and *bad* have a shortest distance between them.

724. *Fear* and *stupidity* are always friends; but bravery and intelligence are not so.

725. Everything can be proved as *nothing*; but the one that proves it so has turned out to be *something*. Since that everything includes something, something becomes nothing; that again proves that the nothing is always something!

726. A *good man* knows more bad than a *bad man* knows about good. Again the bad man knows less bad than the good man about bad. Only the bad man *does* more bad than the good man actually does!

727. *Idiots* never exist alone; they have a natural tendency either to join or collect similar people. Throughout human history idiots constituted a numerical majority. This numerical dominance of *idiots* has been made as *usefulness*! In the social sphere anybody can create anything but sustenance is not possible unless the majority is assumed to be or actually made as idiots. The social institutions like religion, politics, business, celebrity are all came to be sustainable based on this simple fact. The questions whether idiots created them or they are made to suit the idiots are not mutually exclusive! Above all, *idiots think more or less alike and thus making almost everything possible even in any rational society!*

728. There definitely exists a *power* apart from man; to make it greater than or less than him depend on his power, control, application of reason, above all the ability to manage himself! It becomes his individual responsibility.

729. *Lovers*: when quarrels stop then the love has already ceased!

730. *Love* is a chemistry introduced by physics.

731. *Senses* can deceive us but to that extent their existence is evident and that eventually imparts a significant meaning to this phenomenal world.

732. An *angry man* argues only to justify or defend either his self-interest or prejudice, often unconsciously and very often unsuccessfully.

733. *Woman* is the owner of present tense and *man* the future tense; strangely both disown their past tense!

734. An *innocent* woman embodies nature and hence is irresistibly beautiful. An *intelligent* woman has already acquired the beauty. An honest man *likes* the latter and *loves* the former.

735. In *hatred* two of them fight. In *love* only one of them fights, at a time.

736. If a man is intelligent enough to turn towards the natural endowments within him, he becomes a genius; if he turns towards society he becomes prudent. *Genius* happens when his genes attain better compatibility among them. P*rudence* happens due to effective use of 'reason' across other people.

737. *Freedom* is not a destination but an illusion justified by reason. When a man thinks he is free at that very time itself he becomes a slave to something else he desires intensively but is not yet known to him! This way the deception called freedom is misleading even great intellectuals so long as they blindly believed on the *reason*. The glamorous and

captivating *self-determination* is a gambit of reason; self-determination is a circle drawn by reason that too with a small radius. The man within the circle perceives himself as being protected but it actually serves only to suppress his natural lineaments and emotional capacities. No beautiful and sensible things ever happened in such circle of isolation, aloofness, indifference but only with reference to others; therefore, before a man gets freedom the *nature* already ensured a relation.

738. *Love* has to be necessarily and inescapably unconditional, after all the brain is never able to set out any conditions.

739. *Nature* manifests itself better through a woman, a man's interpretation of good or bad happens subsequently.

740. My dear *reason*, when a million nerves work behind human *desire* before he become aware of it on what basis can you claim independence for his decisions? With respect to a human being's decision you are late, but you're the first one to become conscious of it! A man can never understand himself, either through the slow *evolution* of reason or through the prompt response of *meditation* this fact would become clear; that is what he really claims as understanding! Honestly there can be no saints but only human beings with evolving reason that can have a better access to one's inner nature and hence experience. Once inner nature is experienced, again the unique way of his reason subdues and paves way for a different kind of understanding called *intuition*. Further *there is no end to the quest of a human mind: the intuition is a continuous story with big picture while reason being a short story; from the perspective of individual human mind they remain so forever!*

741. Whatever a *human mind* imagines, fantasizes, expects and intends now had already become its creations!

742. A man can only manifest and express himself better, if it suits the world around him, he becomes a *hero* again only for those who couldn't express themselves.

743. A man's *life* is a process of loosing himself in his *mind* with reason being the due witness.

744. A *man* without reason is like a bare *animal* out there; with reason the same animal coalesces 'within' the human being.

745. *Love* is the only lesson that a man of *reason* couldn't rewrite. Love is a blank paper until nature writes something on it for the illiterate man to learn, acquaints himself so that he experiences the existence of the very nature within him. *In love, a man is directly at war with nature, if nature wins love becomes a success and if he wins his love is lost!*

746. *Art* is a highly refined form of lust. It is society that has refined lust just after the concerned individual's genes come to be receptive and responsive to it.

747. *Geography* makes a man and man makes history.

748. Mathematics teaches man abstract ideas, science impose laws, art pleases only to distort the human mind, religion cripples reason, nature laughs, finally the poor man weeps! *A man who cannot understand himself unwittingly allows the 'circumstances' to take the decision on his behalf.*

749. Most of the times not taking the *risk* actually turned out to be a big risk. But the understating this fact happens to

him a bit later. Risk is a great *opportunity* and by taking risks a man may be able to bring a lot of things under his control otherwise he will be silently handled by forces that are not known to him. In brief by avoiding a risk a man only postpones it without any benefit.

750. *Prejudices* in the name of gender, race, caste, nationalism etc. are necessary to justify different levels of *stupidity,* at a particular time across human beings at different places, and at same place at different times!

751. The world as a whole has never changed; only some parts erupt and other parts subside periodically. The very *evolution* is a tiny part of the eruptions that are perceptible to human senses. A human being is still tinier part of that evolution. Therefore a human being is a part of a part of 'that' has never changed! If someone thinks he has changed the world, including a brute revolutionary, he has to only laugh to himself later, at silence.

Conclusion

In this book, I presented many of my thoughts in as concise a way as possible, often only with brief explanations. Some of the *Ideas* like '*nature has no time*' or '*man in single has no culture*' are left to the readers' imaginations. This is because I, with the intention to cover various aspects of human life, decided this ***first*** book of *the trilogy* was to be that way. It is practically not possible even to connect a dozen individual thoughts and make a conclusion in this small book.

However, here I take a few thoughts that are close to my *heart* and of immense practical significance and share them with you for the conclusion of this book. These are about *patience, consciousness, faith* and *reason*.

I consider *patience* as a man's the greatest *virtue* and preceptor. Patience is a worthy property of any really *conscious* man. As such I deal with *patience* and *consciousness* together. In the same way *faith* cannot be deliberated without *reason*. Therefore, I discuss faith and reason together.

Patience **and** ***consciousness***

A man or woman is physical, mental, social, *continuous* and above all *conscious*. A man's very existence means a *conscious* existence; whether he is conscious or not he is mentally continuous! Strangely a man's mind is larger in extent than his own consciousness. As such mentally he is always continuous but only he is conscious and discontinuous in physical terms. He is conscious, throughout his life, of the requirements that arise from the above said spheres of influences, the physical, mental and social etc.

In the course of his conscious existence if the man does not achieve what he 'deserves' he may become socially deviant or fight to realize his rights in legitimate ways or maintain *patience*. The last one out of the three possible actions is of particular importance here, since the discussion is about *patience*. This way *patience is something that pertains to consciousness.* An enormous consciousness precedes human patience. Hence, a conscious man only can attempt to maintain patience.

The idea of patience cannot be meaningfully applied to a child or any animals of a lower order. This is because the child or animal is neither expected to be conscious nor does he/she possess enough mental capacity to understand its rightful requirements. Hence *patience has its origin in the desire of a conscious human being. Patience has no other occasions to come into existence in* the *human mind except when a man becomes conscious of what he deserves but yet to accomplish his dreams and ambitions. As such patience cannot originate if there is no demand to fulfill the requirements, natural or social, of a conscious man!*

A man of *patience* is actually the man who is yet to accomplish his rightful dues. He has to be definitely conscious but can either be mentally too *weak* or should have exceptionally *strong* mental qualities. The former case has little or no consequence because a weak mind hardly retains its intentions for long and hence the actual '*period of patience*' also becomes less. The weak man, though conscious, is not able to hold on to his intentions for long. But the latter one with a strong mind, remembers, retains, preserves and keeps in-hold all of its *intentions* that are not yet satiated. *Such a strong yet patient man is destined to receive in future what he morally 'deserves' in exponentially large proportion in comparison to his actual waiting 'period of patience.'* A brief reasoning of how this happens is given below.

We have to start with the *instinct*. It is a self- evident fact that instinct is universal to all living things including human beings. But in the case of human beings as man evolves simultaneously some part of the instinct develops as *desire*. Rather the instinct is better understood as *desire* because of the well developed consciousness of the human mind. As such the desire is a modification of the instinct to suit the human being as a social animal.

The desire generates *expectations* both good and bad in any given societal setting. The expectations are due to the awareness of things in relation to the social background while the actual accomplishments of the same 'expectations' depend on the pace at which nature itself works. This is because nature is not only continuous but it is blind to the discontinuous existence of the man in question. However the intentions of the discretely existing man are *echoed* in nature through his mind. At this juncture without going into the deeper meaning of how human intentions get echoed in nature, as it will be dealt in greater detail in *book two* and *three* of this series, I take some liberty and jump into the following conclusions.

It is true that a social man is conscious of his discrete existence. As such his mental *expectations* are real. His expectations happen in the practical world and hence are with reference to the things and men around him. Often there is a gap or mismatch in the *time scale* between the expectations of a conscious man backed by societal standards and the pace at which nature works. The man in question is aware of this 'time gap'. If the man did not accomplish what he deserves he is in a *time lag*; if another man reaps the results earlier than his expected time he is in *time rush*.

The 'time lag' and 'time rush' are cyclic process in human fortunes that apparently get reflected in particular social environments. But the very cyclic process is actually created by virtue of the 'continuous nature' of the very blind *nature*. The man in a 'time rush' is not relevant here as the man in the *time lag* only becomes eligible and is expected to be in *patience*. Hence the man in *time lag* is waiting in patience but his intentions never dies. *His intentions spread far beyond his physical realm only to return back to him in abundance and bountiful measure much more than he originally expected.*

Can anyone say the *dirt poor* man in the streets is not eligible to reasonable rights in comparison to a man of ordinary endowments residing in a *mansion* located just few feet away? This social situation cannot be justified by human *reason* only because reason takes into account a brief period of human awareness or consciousness, predominately decided by physical and social necessities. Reason due to such discrete consciousness is indifferent and hence dispenses with the mentally, intentionally continuous nature of human existence. Therefore, within the brief period called 'human life span' the *seemingly* problematic situation cannot be resolved.

In this context only I earlier invoked the idea relating the tracing the genealogy of a king and a beggar. The poor man on the streets is in *time lag* and the man in the mansion is in *time rush*. The graph of the former would steadily rise, if he maintained peace and patience. The graph of latter may inch up little further only to soon fall. The man waiting in patience is more secure in each day ahead than the already secured man! It all presupposes the fact that the human mind is continuous, and only his awareness things are discontinuous.

A man's awareness renders him weak, a little more awareness prepares him to be strong, further and further awareness directs him to maintain *peace and patience. The intentions of a patient man are infinitely powerful. Time does the trick and makes patience the greatest of all virtues. Hence a man of patience is not only the strongest of all; finally he turned out to be the most fortunate one!*

Reason and **faith**

The mind is blind and as enormous as nature. A small portion of *the large* mind attached to human beings also is blind, until reason develops in some corner of it. The *reason* and *faith* are extension of a man's same blind mind. However, the *reason* is bit more developed than faith and further it gets distinguishable due to its ability to ask questions while the faith, an *incipient reason*, tacitly becomes dumb to avoid painful questions. The faith is tacit because it not only indents to escape the questions but as a faith it also intends to become subsequently answers for many more questions!

It is strange, since the reason is always smart in questioning even after knowing very well that it cannot answer. The situation becomes *indeterminate* because the reason is not able to answer such questions. All these happen in human mind of a matured man at sometime or other.

In order to avoid such indeterminate situation only the same reason transforms itself deliberately as faith and becomes blind to the very reasoning process. It desires to play a blind faith, since as a faith it need not answer yet it can make *itself available as answers* to all indeterminate questions created by the reason and couldn't be replied by the same reason earlier. This way a reason plays *dual roles* in the world of practice: morning as reason and evening as faith, as a reason to young man and as a faith to far aged man and so on either to satisfy or to save a troubled human mind.

Therefore the *reason* and *faith* are different interpretations of the reason only. As the result of differing interpretations necessitated by varied mental circumstances both the reason and faith are understood *permanently* as two distinct if not opposing perspectives of human nature. But in reality both are in *connection*, however inconspicuous the connection may be, and are never two distinct and discrete mental faculties.

Here is a real world example: a man has two sons. The *elder* one is very obedient and always assists his parents and hence his father supports, likes, loves and grieves him according to his needs and difficulties; also the father becomes aware of his son's dependency on him. The *younger* son is not as close to his father as the elder one. The young son tries to face the world on his own yet not successful all the times. He learns, manages, struggles and builds himself strong only with occasional help from his father. Slowly and steadily the younger son overcomes the distress and obstacles of the external world both natural and social. This way he acquires sufficient strength due to the awareness of nature and society and able to go beyond his own inhibitions to guide not only his elder brother and father but also the surrounding society.

His father is really proud of the young son's strength and his usefulness to the society. Here the father is *mind* the elder brother is the *faith* and the younger one is the *reason*. But in reality these three are not distinct entities functioning in their own discrete ways. The human mind is the base and the faith and reason are extension of mind and always in continuity with the very mind.

Further, if one watches the massive fire ball of the sun, he can witness the erupting sun flares of differing heights on its surface; some flares are low and other are very high extending to thousands of kilometers. Since the flares are only extensions of the sun they are sucked back into sun due to its gravity. This happens all the time. *If a human mind is analogous to the sun then the faith and reason are akin to the eruption of the low and high flares respectively; the faith and reason are only extensions of mind and hence they again fall back into human mind due to its enormity.* While faith roams closer to the mind, young reason wanders for a little extra mile, like the high sun flares, before returning home; only during this brief moment does reason appear to be a self-determining and independent faculty within the human mind, much in the same way a fish can claim independence from the ocean during the brief period of jumping above the ocean surface before necessarily falling back into the same ocean! The fate of reason is necessarily linked to the human mind, like a fish to the ocean. The same reason, as *faith,* deliberately does not want independence but as a *reason* it has full *faith* in itself and does not admit its dependence, on the necessities of human mind.

Thus both faith and reason are one and the same thing. They behave some times as *faith* and some other time as *reason* only to suit the numerous plights and predicaments of the mind to which they are attached. The *one* that renders the mind such adverse conditions is the *instinct*; ultimately the mind, faith, reason all works only to satisfy the underlying master, the instinct. *These different ways of a mind's behaviors to satisfy the instinct apparently manifest sometime as faith and some other times as reason.*

Again to reiterate, the faith and reason are one and the same: if the reason is able to provide answers to its own questions it claims credit and distinguishes itself as science, logic etc, if the questions are not able to be answered the frail yet tricky reason bundles 'all that questions' as religion and declares itself to be faith!

Faith is a decrepit, infirm and subdued form of reason and reason is a stable, substantial and sound faith. Both reason and faith evolve all the time, albeit the latter being slow; at the back of the human mind both are born as one and the same thing but brought up as different entities, often both are projected as the direct opposite of and also as antagonistic to each other only to suit the discreteness and discriminations, the inevitable presumptions of this phenomenal world.

If the god atop a hill temple is the destination, the steps leading to the temple are the *reason* and the steps bring back down is the *faith*. Steps are same, but the concerned man's mental states are different; while climbing up the reason is so weak hence instructs the human mind to entrust a part or entire responsibility on god and on return it gained enough strength to be able to apportion a *part* of its own responsibility and bestowing the remaining portion to the god! At the temple weak reason is tactical and transforms into faith. *As such reason is never a destination but is the best of all possible means*. It is reason that convinces the human mind and leads it in a direction best known to it; only at the end of the journey does reason realize its own limit, rather it reveals to human mind its duress. This is what happens to the human mind at all desperate and consequential circumstances, after led by the young warrior; it happens in *worship*, in *war* and in *love*. The warrior turns into a peacemaker.

A man's life is nothing more than a frequent inter-play of his *reason* and his own *mental experiences* that are understandable yet beyond the control of that very reason! This way human reason knows as much weakness as its own strength.

"Reason is the torch bearer of the human mind. In which direction the torch leads is known only when the torch itself dims and discharges. When the charge of the torch is drained, the disabled reason transforms itself as faith and leaves the mind in obscurity and darkness. But soon the mind left blind by reason in external darkness without any direction receives instruction from within, internally in the form of intuition, on what to rely on; during this brief period of darkness reason does a makeover as intuition! The situation makes reason to lie low only to transform as faith that readily permits the intuition waiting not far way. Now, the source of guidance for human mind shifts from brain to the heart!

As such the presence, absence and transformation of reason is really its many avatars that conduct a human mind. Reason conducts a man in either direction, towards development or destruction, only to write its own conclusion. To know whether reason is a boon or a bane is conditioned by the experiences of a conscious individual mind and hence left to the judgment of that individual."